SHOP IMAGE GRAPHICS

in Paris

Living, FASHION, FOOD, service

SHOP IMAGE GRAPHICS
in Paris

PIE BOOKS

2-32-4 Minami-Otsuka, Toshima-ku, Tokyo 170-0005 Japan
Tel: +81-3-5395-4811 Fax: +81-3-5395-4812 http://www.piebooks.com
e-mail: editor@piebooks.com e-mail: sales@piebooks.com

ISBN978-4-89444-704-2 Printed in Japan

Foreword

本書は、インテリアとグラフィックデザインが統一されたイメージでつくり上げられた、ショップのアイデンティティデザインを紹介している。

今回取り上げたのは、伝統と先端のモードが混在する都市パリ。パリという街が、長い歴史のなかでつくり上げた数々の美しい建築やモチーフをパリの人々は愛し、そしてそれを時代の形に変化させて新たなクリエイティブを生み出している。この連鎖的につながっていくクリエイティブは、パリに住み、パリでものをつくる人たちの特権ともいえよう。パリには、強烈な個性を持つ店が並んでいるが、大きく3つの傾向が見られる。伝統に新たなクリエイティブを吹き込んだもの、世界のトップクリエイターによる斬新なアイデアのデザイン。そして小さいながらも、これまでにないオリジナリティを持った新しいタイプのショップである。

伝統的なモチーフを新しい形で表現し、成功しているのはラデュレ (p.114) のパッケージシリーズであろう。一見クラシカルに見えるモチーフは、美しい色と組み合わせることにより新しい息吹が吹き込まれ、パリの名店にふさわしいパッケージデザインとなっている。古い建築を活かしたインテリアでありながら、最新のクリエイティブと食の形を提供しているテイクアウトフードのコジャン (p.122) や食器店のアスティエ・ドゥ・ヴィラット (p.024) もまた、伝統を活かし独自のクリエイションを生み出しているといえるだろう。
デザインの先端という意味では、モード界の帝王、クリスチャン・ラクロワによるゴージャスを極めたデザインホテル オテル・デュ・プティ・ムーラン (p.168) やパリのエスプリを思わせる、シャンタル・トーマスによるランジェリーショップ (p.068)、そしてフィリップ・スタルクのデザインによる近未来的なレストラン コング (p.142) など、モードとデザインを先導するパリの存在を確固たるものにしている。
またそれとは対照的に、等身大のデザインながらも個性を光らせる書店のラ・ココット (p.028) や公衆トイレでさえも美しくデザインしてしまったポワン・ヴェー・セー (p.183) はこれからのパリを面白いものにしてくれそうな若いエネルギーが感じられるショップといえる。

どこを切り取っても斬新でオリジナリティのあるパリのショップデザインには、オーナーのポリシーそしてパリの人々のポリシーを感じさせられる、他の都市には真似のできないデザインであることは明らかである。

最後になりましたが、本書制作にあたり、快く取材と素材の提供にご協力くださったショップオーナーの方々に、この場をかりて深くお礼を申し上げます。

ピエ・ブックス編集部

This book showcases examples of imaginative shop identity design characterized by the coordination of interiors and graphics.

Our focus here is on Paris – a city where tradition mingles with cutting-edge fashion. Parisians love the myriad of beautiful buildings and motifs born out of their city's long centuries of history, and enjoy altering them in new and creative ways in accordance with the needs and aesthetics of the times. Perhaps this chain of creativity is a special privilege of those who live in Paris, and make things in Paris. The French capital is full of shops of intensely individual impact, but broadly speaking, three tendencies in shop design can be observed. These are shops that breathe new creativity into tradition; designs based on the innovative ideas of some of the world's top creative people; and a new kind of shop that while small, displays a quirky originality.

The Ladurée packaging series (p.114) is one successful example of a new take on a traditional motif. A breath of fresh air produced by combination with attractive colours blows through what at first glance seems a classical motif, in a package design perfect for a venerable Parisian institution. The likes of the takeout food store Cojean (p.122), which offers the latest in creative flair and inventive food amid surroundings that utilize the best features of old buildings, and tableware emporium Astier de Villatte (p.024), take tradition and add inspired creativity to magnificent effect.
The Hotel du Petit Moulin (p.168), the ornate design hotel by king of fashion – certainly when it comes to cutting-edge design – Christian Lacroix; the lingerie shop by Chantal Thomass (p.068), and the futuristic Restaurant Kong with design courtesy of Philippe Starck (p.142) all help to consolidate Paris's status as a leader of fashion and design.
In contrast, places like the bookshop La Cocotte (p.028), an example of design that is of practical, human proportions yet big on personality, and Point WC (p.183), where even a public toilet has been given the full designer treatment, exude a youthful energy that promises to make Paris an even more exciting place.

One could pick almost any shop design in Paris and find imagination and originality, evidence that here is a city that excels in inimitable design: an expression of the philosophy of Paris shopowners, and the people of Paris.

Finally, allow us to take this opportunity to thank the many shopowners who kindly allowed us to include their premises and supplied material for the book.

PIE BOOKS editors

Contents

Living

Contents

FASHION

Contents

food

Contents

SERVICE

Editorial Notes

Credit format

A	ショップ名	Shop Name
B	制作スタッフ・クレジット	Creative Stuff
C	業種	Type of Business
D	店舗所在地	Address
E	ウェブサイト・アドレス	Web Site Address
F	ショップ・コンセプト文	Shop Description

Creative Stuff

AF:	建築設計事務所	Architectual Firm
A:	ショップ設計者	Architect in Charge
CD:	クリエイティブ・ディレクター	Creative Director
AD:	アート・ディレクター	Art Director
D:	デザイナー	Designer
LD:	ロゴ・デザイナー	Logo Designer
P:	フォトグラファー	Photographer
I:	イラストレーター	Illustrator
CW:	コピーライター	Copywriter
DF:	グラフィック・デザイン事務所	Design Firm

＊上記以外の制作者呼称は省略せずに記載しております。
Full name of all others involved in the creation / production of the work.

＊本書に掲載されている店舗写真、販促ツール、商品、店名、住所などは、すべて2008年7月時点での情報になります。ご了承ください。
All in store-related information, including photography, promotional items, products, shop name, and address are accurate as of December 2006.

＊作品提供者の意向によりクレジット・データの一部を記載していないものがあります。
Please note that some credit data has been omitted at the request of the submittor.

LIVING

Living

Living

Blanc D'Ivoire

A:Manuel OPDENAKKER　CD,AD,LD:Monic FISCHER

ブラン・ディヴォワール
homeware インテリア用品
25, rue de Saintonge 75003 Paris
http://www.blancdivoire.com

Shopping Bag
ショッピングバッグ

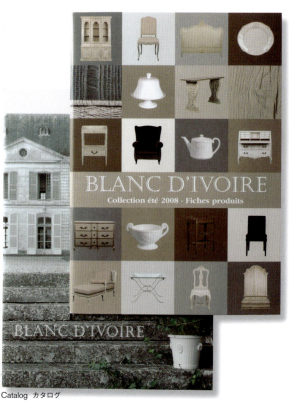

Catalog カタログ

An interior décor brand started by Frenchwoman Monique Fichet who worked for many years in the fashion industry. As you can tell from the name Blanc d'Ivoire (the white of ivory), the store has a range of natural chic items in soft colours that are enormously popular among lovers of French style including Parisians. The new store opened in the North Le Marais district that is described as a launch pad for fashion trends is spaciously laid out over three floors to form a kind of "world of brands."

長くモードの世界で仕事をしてきたフランス人女性、モニク・フィシェさんが始めたインテリアのブランド。「象牙の白」というネーミングからも感じられるように、ソフトな色調によるナチュラルシックなアイテムを展開。パリジェンヌをはじめ、フレンチスタイルを愛する人々の間で絶大な人気がある。流行の発信地ともいわれる北マレ地区に新しくオープンしたショップは、3フロアをゆうゆうと使って、ブランドワールドを一堂に展開した形になっている。

Shop Card　ショップカード

Post Card
ポストカード

Leaflet　リーフレット

Au Nom de la Rose

オー・ノム・ドゥ・ラ・ローズ
florist フラワーショップ
7, avenue Mozart 75016 Paris
http://www.aunomdelarose.fr

P:Christian PONCELET

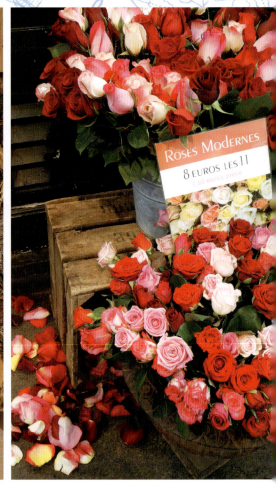

Sticker
ステッカー

Shop Card
ショップカード

Message Card
メッセージカード

Leaflet
リーフレット

All the shops have the same leaf mark on the dark-green façade and the shop name in white lettering. The displays that reach as far as the sidewalk outside the shop are inlaid with rose petals. Generous quantities of petals are also placed in the shopping bags used for wrapping the bouquets and floral arrangements, an effective way of creating a memorable shop image.

「バラの名のもとに」というネーミングのフラワーチェーン。いずれのショップも、深緑色のファサードと白で描かれた店名と葉のマークは共通。加えて、舗道にまで広がるディスプレイにはいつもバラの花びらがちりばめられている。花びらは、ブーケやアレンジメントを入れたショッピングバッグの中にもふんだんにあしらわれ、ショップイメージを印象づける効果も発揮している。

Au Nom de la Rose

100 g

Package パッケージ

014

Les Touristes

A,CD,LD:Yann GICQUEL / Jérôme GIGOT

レ・トゥーリスト
fabric, miscellaneous goods
布、雑貨
17, rue des Blancs Manteaux 75004 Paris
http://www.lestouristes.eu

A miscellaneous goods store in the Le Marais district. In addition to the shirts, gowns, bags, accessory holders, lamp shades made in the Les Touristes signature cotton print, Les Touristes offers a range Asian-style miscellaneous goods that have a kind of kitsch charm. The brightly coloured walls and window displays create a cozy atmosphere that makes the customers smile.

マレ地区にある雑貨店。オリジナルのコットンプリントによって作られたシャツ、ガウン、バッグ、小物入れ、ランプシェードなどのほか、ノスタルジックでどことなくキッチュな魅力があるアジアンテイストの雑貨などが並ぶ。カラフルなカラーコンビネーションによる壁やウィンドーのディスプレイには、見る人を微笑ませるような、ほのぼのとした雰囲気がある。

Tag
商品タグ

015

Perigot

A,CD,AD,LD：Frédéric PERIGOT

ペリゴー

miscellaneous goods 生活雑貨
16, boulevard des Capucines 75009 Paris
http://www.perigot.fr

SPRAY
EN INOX

GRAND MODÈLE
19,50 EUROS

PETIT MODÈLE
16,50 EUROS

Pour humidifier vos
cheveux, pour les
produits d'entretiens,
pour vaporiser vos
plantes...

PERIGOT®

TORCHON
A VAISSELLE
« ŒILLET »

10,00 EUROS

Attention, pas pour les
ventes !!

A miscellaneous goods brand produced by Frederic Perigot, a top name in the world of French design. Based on the philosophy that the more skillful the design, the longer the life of the collection, he has designed a range of items that are useful in the various scenes of everyday life including everyday items and travel goods, all based on a universal design concept that transcends the male-female divide and fashion trends. The window display that changes on a regular basis is what you would expect from a designer's boutique.

フランスのデザイン界を代表するひとり、フレデリック・ペリゴー氏による雑貨のブランド。「デザインが巧妙であるほど、コレクションの寿命は長い」という哲学のもとに、性別も流行も超越した普遍的なデザインコンセプトで、日用品、旅行グッズなど、日常の生活のさまざまなシーンで有益なものを作り出している。定期的にがらりと様変わりするウィンドーディスプレイも、デザイナーブティックならではだ。

Perigot

Sticker
ステッカー

www.perigot.fr

Memopads メモパッド

Shop Card
ショップカード

PERIGOT
16, BOULEVARD DES CAPUCINES
75009 PARIS
TEL + 33 (0) 1 53 40 98 90
Ⓜ MADELEINE OU OPERA

15, RUE DU DRAGON
75006 PARIS
TEL + 33 (0) 1 45 44 01 73
Ⓜ ST GERMAIN DES PRES

GALERIE LE CARROUSEL DU LOUVRE
99, RUE DE RIVOLI
75001 PARIS
TEL + 33 (0) 1 42 60 10 85

www.perigot.fr

Papier +

CD:Denis BRUNET

パピエ・プリュス
paper products 紙製品
9, rue de Pont Louis Philippe 75004 Paris
http://www.papierplus.com

Sticker
ステッカー

Shop Card
ショップカード

PAPIER +
www.papierplus.com

The street that connects to the Louis Philippe Bridge leading to Île Saint Louis in the Le Marais district on the Right Bank is packed with shops dealing in paper products. One of these shops, Papier, has been around since 1976. Since the book-like notebooks that established Papier's reputation in the early days, the style of the product range has continued to develop as times have changed and is now a colourful range of stationery items including albums, storage boxes and binders produced in paper and fabric.

パリ右岸のマレ地区、サンルイ島へとかかるルイ・フィリップ橋につながる通りは、紙製品を扱う店が軒を連ねる。この店もそのうちの一軒で、1976年から営業。初期のころに評判をよんだ、本のような体裁のノートから、時代ともに作風の発展を重ね続け、アルバム、整理用のボックス、バインダーなど種々のステイショナリーアイテムを吟味した紙と布でカラフルに展開している。

Odorantes

A,CD,AD,LD:Emmanuel SAMMARTINO, Christophe HERVE

オドラン
florist フラワーショップ
9, rue Madame 75006 Paris

A space decorated in the colours of black and grey, the antique furniture and art objets … the flowers decorated with stuffed toy birds that are part of two owners' collection resemble actors standing on the stage of a theatre. At Odorantes, 80% of the flowers are roses, grown in the suburbs of Paris. The finely rolled sheets of paper containing poems that are attached to the bows on the bouquets are a tasteful embodiment of the aesthetic sensibility of the two owners.

黒とグレーを基調にした空間、アンティークの家具やオブジェ、そしてオーナー2人のコレクションである剥製の鳥たちにも飾られた花々は、まるでテアトルの舞台にたつ役者のよう。花はその8割がバラで、それもパリ近郊で栽培されたものというように、徹底したこだわりに貫かれたショップである。花束の結び目には、ポエムが書かれた紙を細く丸めて添えるという心憎い演出もまた、彼ら2人の審美眼を具現化している。

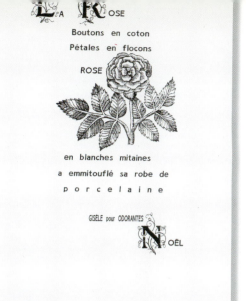

LA ROSE

Boutons en coton
Pétales en flocons
ROSE

en blanches mitaines
a emmitouflé sa robe de
porcelaine

GISÈLE pour ODORANTES
NOËL

JEU...

la cultiver vous honorer
la voler vous combler
la cueillir vous l'offrir
...DE ROSES

gisèle pour ODORANTES

AMOUREUSEMENT... ROSE

vous perdre

dans mes bras

serait une injure

à votre éclat

vous y retrouver

plus digne

de votre beauté

gisèle pour ODORANTES

Poem 詩

Rose glammouR

en robe de Pompadour

dentelle ses pétales

et se pourpre les joues

de graines de beauté

gisèle pour ODORANTES

Decorative Stamps 切手状の飾り

Sticker
ステッカー

Shop Card
ショップカード

9 rue madame
75006
Paris
ODORANTES
tél fax
42 84 03 00

Lentou

CD.AD:Pierre ROMANET

セントゥ
home accessories インテリア雑貨
26, boulevard Raspail 75007 Paris
http://www.sentou.fr

Envelope 封筒

Post Card ポストカード

Shop Card
ショップカード

A pioneer home accessories store in Paris that incorporates contemporary design items into our daily lives and is always one step ahead of the times. Le Sentou is well known for adding must-have items such as Isamu Noguchi lamps to its inventory before anyone else. In the store filled with the work of popular designers including 100drine and Tsé & Tsé associées, there is also a temporary expo corner.

生活のなかにコンテンポラリーなデザインのアイテムを取り入れるという、時代の潮流のさきがけになった、いわばパリのインテリアセレクトショップのさきがけ的存在。イサム・ノグチのランプなどをいち早くレパートリーに加えたことでも知られている。100drine、Tsé & Tsé associéesなど、いまをときめくデザイナーたちの作品であふれたショップには、期間限定のエキスポコーナーなどもある。

Catalog カタログ

Astier de Villatte

A.AD.CD:Ivan PERICOLI, Benoit ASTIER de VILLATTE

アスティエ・ドゥ・ヴィラット
tableware, miscellaneous goods
テーブルウェア、家具
173, rue Saint Honoré 75001 Paris
http://www.astierdevillatte.com

Shop Card
ショップカード

The unique tableware fired using the clay from the suburbs of Paris is highly contemporary but also has a certain nostalgic flavour, and is already a favourite among the discerning population. Astier de Villatte is a shop where such people are in their element, a space created by the wooden furniture and the simple, understated walls. The store is a fine example of maximizing what remained of old store that used to sell artists' paints and giving it a modern twist in the centre of Paris.

パリ近郊の土を用いて焼成されるという食器は、このうえなくコンテンポラリーでありつつ、どこかなつかしいような肌合いをもつ独特なもの。高感度の人々の間では、すでによく知られたアイテムになっている。それらが並ぶショップは、使い込んだ木の家具や、わびた趣の壁がつくる空間。かつて顔料などを扱っていたという歳月を経た店の遺構が、パリの真ん中で現代の感性で生かされているという好例。

Sticker
ステッカー

Astier de Villatte

Post Card　ポストカード

Catalog　カタログ

Pinceloup

A.CD,AD:Couli JOBERT I,LD:Coline ROY-CAMILLE

パンスルー
pet accessories ペット用品
53, quai des Grands Augustins 75006 Paris
http://www.pinceloup.fr

Tag
商品タグ

Ribbon リボン

Leaflet
リーフレット

A store situated on the left bank of the Seine near Pont Neuf for pets and the people who love their pets, Pinceloup was started by a mother with a long career in fashion who had also produced for Hermes and her graphic designer daughter. The original Pinceloup items in red and white striped cotton and the range of pet-related products selected from around the world are displayed elegantly, as you would expect from a mother and daughter with artistic natures.

モードの世界でキャリアを積み、エルメスの商品の制作も手がけているという母と、グラフィストである娘が始めた、ペットとそれを愛する人々のためのショップ。ポンヌフにもほど近い、セーヌ左岸にある。赤と白の縞々のコットンを使ったアイテムなどのオリジナルグッズと、世界中からよりすぐったペット関連の品々が、芸術家肌の母娘ならではのおしゃれなディスプレイで陳列されている。

La Cocotte

A.CD.AD.LD:Andréa WAINER, Nathalie REDARD, Laetitia BERTRAND

ラ・ココット
bookshop, salon de thé
本、雑貨、サロンドテ
5, rue Paul Bert 75011 Paris
http://www.lacocotte.net

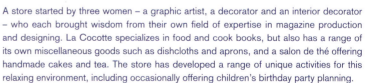

Egg Stand
エッグスタンド

A store started by three women – a graphic artist, a decorator and an interior decorator – who each brought wisdom from their own field of expertise in magazine production and designing. La Cocotte specializes in food and cook books, but also has a range of its own miscellaneous goods such as dishcloths and aprons, and a salon de thé offering handmade cakes and tea. The store has developed a range of unique activities for this relaxing environment, including occasionally offering children's birthday party planning.

グラフィスト、デコレーター、インテリアデコレーションのスタイリストの3人の女性が、雑誌の企画やデザインルームとしてのそれぞれの得意分野の知恵を持ち寄って始めたショップ。料理、味覚にまつわる本を専門とする書店であり、布巾やエプロンなどのオリジナルの雑貨を手がけ、手作りのお菓子とともにお茶をサービスするというサロンドテでもある。肩肘はらずにくつろげるようなこの場所では、ときに子供の誕生パーティの企画を提供するなど、独自の活動を繰り広げている。

***la cocotte *** librairie du goût
5 rue Paul Bert 75011 Paris ✳ 09 54 73 17 77
www.lacocotte.net ✳ andrea@lacocotte.net
Ouvert du mardi au samedi de 10h30 à 20h ✳ Mercredi de 10h30 à 19h
métro Faidherbe Chaligny (ligne 8)

Shop Card
ショップカード

Wrapping Paper
ラッピングペーパー

13 à Table

A:Pascal BILDSTEIN

トレーズ・ア・ターブル
kitchenware, tableware キッチン
34, rue de Rivoli 75004 Paris
http://www.13atable.com

Leaflet
リーフレット

Sticker
ステッカー

cuisinez, décorez, recevez!

Wrapping Paper
ラッピングペーパー

The slogan "Cook, decorate, host" is repeated on the store's shopping bags and on the floor in front of the cash registers. As the slogan suggests, 13 à table offers kitchen utensils and miscellaneous goods for setting and decorating your table. The store's three floors are full of ideas and a variety of exciting products for coordinating your table. A cooking school has been set up in a section of the store to comprehensively fulfill all customers' cooking and kitchen requirements.

ショッピングバッグにも、レジ前の床にも繰り返されている言葉「料理して、飾って、迎え入れる」。それが示すとおり、台所用品とテーブル周り、そしてデコレーションのための雑貨を扱うショップ。3フロアの店内は、テーブルコーディネートのアイデアがわきそうなさまざまなアイテムで埋め尽くされている。また一部には、料理教室も併設されていて、キッチンの多方面のニーズにこたえられるショップになっている。

Côté Bastide

A,AD,CD,LD:Nicole HOUQUES

コテ・バスティッド
miscellaneous goods, fragrances
インテリア雑貨、フレグランス
4, rue de Poissy 75005 Paris
http://www.cotebastide.com

Shop Card
ショップカード

Envelope 封筒

A bastide is the villa or country house peculiar to the south of France. This maison that is based in Aix-en-Provence abounds with an atmosphere that is simple and liberating yet has exquisite taste, as the name suggests, created in the landscape of the south of France. Enhancing the simple yet high-quality linen and the coordination of furniture is the attention to detail. The room colognes, powders and soaps in their superb packaging alone make a memorable impression.

バスティッドとは、南フランス独特の別荘や田舎家を示す言葉。エクサンプロヴァンスに母体をもつこのメゾンは、そのネーミングのとおり、南仏の風土に育まれた、素朴で開放的な、それでいて趣味のよい雰囲気にあふれている。シンプルで上質なリネンや家具によるコーディネーションをさらに引き立てるのが細部へのこだわり。パッケージングも秀逸なルームコロンやパウダー、石鹸類はそれだけでも存在感のあるアイテムとなっている。

Catalog カタログ

Leaflet
リーフレット

La Compagnie de Provence

A:Samuel FRICAUD, ENDEMIQUE CONCEPT

ラ・カンパニー・ドゥ・プロヴァンス
soap, cosmetics
石けん、コスメティック用品
16, rue Vignon 75009 Paris
http://www.lcdpmarseille.com

Savon de Marseilles in a plain, square block used to be in every bathroom in every home in France. It developed from there to become a brand product successfully establishing a bold brand image with successive releases of new products wrapped in attractive packaging. In the shop that looks like a pure white box, the colourful range of cosmetic products have been arranged in an orderly manner around the shop and interspersed with colourful duck objets.

昔はフランスのどの家庭の水場にもあったというほど親しまれてきた、飾り気のない四角いブロックのようなマルセイユの石鹸。そこから発展して、現在では次々と魅力的なパッケージをまとった新商品を発表するブランドとして、大胆なイメージチェンジに成功した。真っ白な箱のようなショップには、カラフルな色で展開されたコスメティック製品が整然と並び、カラフルなアヒルのオブジェが愛嬌を添えている。

SAVON DE
MARSEILLE
EXTRA PUR
MARSEILLE
S O A P

Package
パッケージ

Package
パッケージ

13
LCDPLUXE

www.lcdpmarseille.com

LCDP
LA COMPAGNIE
DE PROVENCE
MARSEILLE

Pylones

A,CD,AD:PYLONES TEAM

ピローヌ
miscellaneous goods 雑貨
c/c des 3 Quartiers 23, boulevard de
la Madeleine 75001 Paris
http://www.pylones.com

Package パッケージ

Shopping Bag
ショッピングバッグ

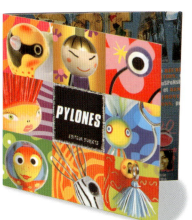

Miscellaneous goods, produced in vivid colours with motifs of animals and insects. As well as being practical, they abound with that sense of fun that brings to life the world of naïve imagination of our childhood, each item conveying the joy of its creation. The wrapping paper and shopping bags also are as individualistic as the products on offer.

動物や昆虫などのモチーフをふんだんに使いながら、ビビッドなカラーリングで展開される雑貨。それらはいずれも、実用にたえるものでありながら、子供のころの無邪気な想像の世界を形にしたような遊び心にあふれており、アイテムのひとつひとつからクリエーションの楽しさが伝わってくる。ラッピングペーパーやショッピングバッグもまた、商品の存在感に負けないくらい個性に満ちている。

Boutique Assouline

CD,A:Prosper ASSOULINE

ブティック・アスリーヌ

bookshop 本、雑貨

35, rue Bonaparte 75006 Paris
http://www.assouline.com

Bookmark
しおり

A bookstore in the centre of Saint Germain des Prés that has been around since 2005. The parent organization is a publishing company and the books on sale here are produced by the company. The store is full of the art and fashion luxury books that are the mainstay of the company, the types of books that are almost objets in themselves. Collections of books in leather-bound cases produced in collaboration with the Chanel, Coach and Goyard brands are also available. Assouline is always on the lookout for new and fresh challenges.

サンジェルマンデプレの真ん中に2005年お目見えした書店。母体は出版社で、ここにあるのはすべてがそのメゾンの編集によるもの。アートやモード関連の豪華本がほとんどで、それ自体がすでにオブジェともいえそうな本がびっしりと並んでいる。また、シャネル、コーチ、ゴヤールといったブランドとコラボレートした、革張りのケースに入ったシリーズなども手がけ、新しい試みにも挑戦している。

ASSOULINE

FALL COLLECTION 2007

Catalog　カタログ

66Assouline Publishing prints books
that are like literary binoculars—glossy portals
to the rarefied realms of high society.99
MEN'S VOGUE, FEBRUARY 2007

66Assouline has become the fashion
industry's favorite publisher
for books that are beautiful,
splashy and highly flattering.99
LOS ANGELES TIMES, JANUARY 2007

66Book Publisher Assouline
is a darling of the fashion world
with its tomes on style,
design and art and its chicly
minimal stores.99
WWD, FEBRUARY 2007

66Creating the glossiest
coffee-table books around
has turned Assouline into a luxury brand,
one that its founders are intent on expanding.99
W MAGAZINE, JANUARY 2007

www.assouline.com

Opening October 2007
ASSOULINE NEW YORK
The Plaza
768 Fifth Avenue
New York, NY

ASSOULINE PARIS
35, rue Bonaparte
Paris VI - France
Tel. : 00 33 (0)1 43 29 23 20

66About America's citizenry,
American fashion has always seemed
to have an almost prodigal ability
to absorb its disparate creative sources
and expressions into a collective whole.99

The Assouline Lifetime Collection

94

6 x 8'' / 15 x 21 cm · 48€

Olivier Pitou

Fleuriste

Shop Card
ショップカード

Match
マッチ

Olivier Pitou's shop has an interior that would never be described as large, yet the mountains of flowers stretch to the back of the store, creating a dreamlike world inside a tunnel of flowers. Using sneaker laces imprinted with the shop's logo to tie the bouquets of flowers is an example of the attention to detail. On the opposite side of the street is a high-quality grocer with the same owner with matches that have the same bumble bee trademark.

決して広いとはいえない店内だが、たわわな花々はこんもりとした小山をつくり、店の奥までびっしりと連なって、まるで花のトンネルのなかにでもいるような夢のような世界を作り出している。花束のラッピングには、店のロゴがプリントされたスニーカーの紐を使うなど、細部へのこだわりもある。通りの向かいには、同じオーナーによる高級食材店があり、ここでもトレードマークの蜂があしらわれたマッチなどを置いている。

Pierre Frey

A.CD.AD:Patrick FREY

ピエール・フレイ
interior fabrics インテリアファブリック
2, rue de Furstenberg 75006 Paris
http://www.pierrefrey.com

Post Card
ポストカード

Ribbon
リボン

This store is the first name that comes to mind among interior fabric stores in Paris. In the Saint Germain neighborhood on the Left Bank, shops selling products such as cushions and bedcovers and lampshades and also furniture dealers are located next to fabric showrooms to create a large "world of brands."

パリのインテリアファブリックの店としてまず名前が挙がるのが、この店。左岸のサンジェルマン界隈では、布そのもののショールームに隣接して、クッションやベッドカバー、ランプシェードなどの製品によって構成されたショップ、また家具を扱うショップが隣り合わせていて、一大ブランドワールドを形成している。

Marianne Robic

マリアンヌ・ロビック
florist フラワーショップ
39, rue de Babylone 75007 Paris

The shop belonging to Marianne Robic, a talented female florist from among the members of the Parisian florist community. Many of the flowers, which are delivered on a daily basis, are displayed in transparent containers that show off the flowers' freshly cut stems. The displays in the glass-enclosed store window transition in tempo with a carefully considered pitch and balance of colour such as you would see in a masterpiece painting or a flower garden, pleasing to the eyes of children on their way to school or the passengers in a passing bus.

パリのフローリスト仲間の間でも一目おかれる実力派の女性フローリスト、マリアンヌ・ロビックさんの店。毎日のように仕入れる花々の多くは、透明の容器に入れて陳列され、常にみずみずしい切り口をみせている。一面ガラス張りのショーウィンドーはさながら絵画の大作、あるいは花園のように、高低、配色のバランスがよく考えられた、緩急の変化のあるディスプレイで、通学の子供たちや、通りのバスの乗客たちの目を楽しませている。

Tag
商品タグ

Flamant

フラマン
homeware インテリア用品
8, rue Furstemberg, 8, rue de l'Abbaye
75006 Paris
http://www.flamant.com

Menu
メニュー

Package
パッケージ

EAU DU HOME

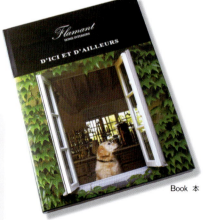

Book 本

The spacious L-shaped store interior has been divided into sections, and the merchandise displayed to make customers feel as if they were actually visiting somebody's home, and also to create a calm and relaxed shopping environment. There is a paint corner with a wide range of paints, a flower shop, and interior design book corner, all with that urban sophistication.

広々としたL字型の店内は、いくつかのパーツに分けられ、ウッディなダイニングキッチン、シックなリビング等々、実際にだれかの家を訪ねているかのようなつくりこんだ丁寧なディスプレイがされていて、ゆったりと落ち着いた雰囲気のなかでショッピングが楽しめる。また種類も豊富なペンキのコーナー、フラワーショップ、インテリア関連の本のコーナーもあり、そのいずれもが都会的で洗練されている。

Gift Box ギフトボックス

Caravane Chambre19/ Emporium

A,CD,AD,LD:Françoise DORGET

キャラヴァン・シャンブル・ディズヌフ／アンポリウム
furniture, miscellaneous
homeware, miscellaneous goods
インテリア、雑貨
19, 22 rue Saint Nicolas 75012 Paris
http://www.caravane.fr

Ribbon
リボン

Ribbon
リボン

Wrapping Paper
ラッピングペーパー

The sister store of the interiors store opened in the Le Marais in 1995. Chambre 19 concentrates mainly on bedroom décor and offers a range of products from countries including North Africa and India where producing things by hand is still common. The miscellaneous goods in the Emporium store opposite Chambre 19 have come from the same countries. The colourful, stylish products that are fun even just to look at were produced as part of a scheme to support poorer regions of the world.

1995年、マレにオープンしたインテリアの店の姉妹店。Chambre19は、寝室のインテリアが中心で、北アフリカやインドなど、手仕事によるもの作りがいまだ盛んな国々で制作した、肌触りのいい布による商品が並ぶ。向かいにあるEmporiumは、同じ地域で作られた雑貨の店。カラフルに、センスよくディスプレイされた、見ているだけでも楽しくなるような空間。

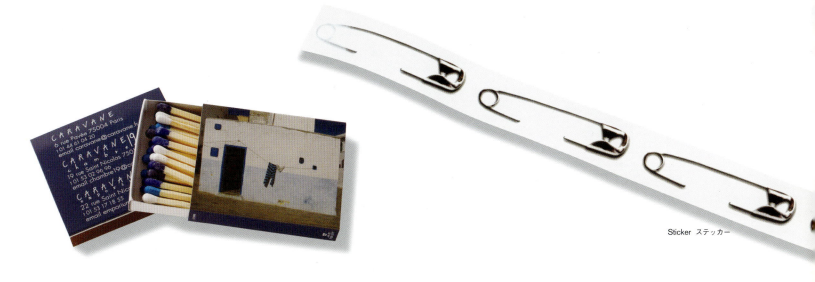

Sticker ステッカー

CARAVANE
meubles en fer

Atoll

Tables Atoll 65×160×38 cm • 65×136×38 cm • 55×81×38 cm

Leka

Miroirs Leka 33×70 cm • 43×98 cm • 55×140 cm

Thali

Tables Thali 45×140×25 cm • 60×180×25 cm
avec plateau coulissant

Hampi

Tables Hampi 40×40×40 cm
empilables

Domino

Tables Domino 35×35×38 cm • 35×70×35 cm

Catalog カタログ

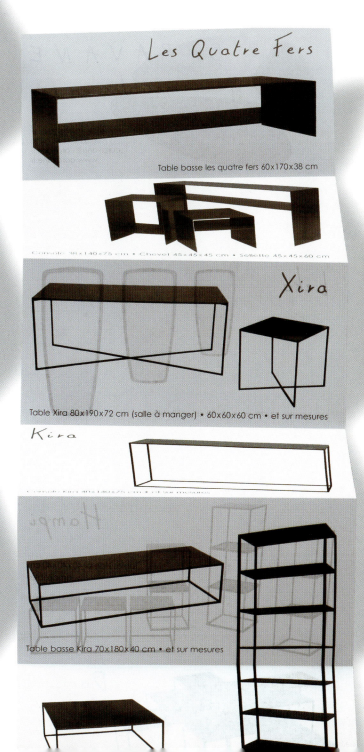

Les Quatre Fers

Table basse les quatre fers 60×170×38 cm

Console 38×140×75 cm • Chevet 45×45×45 cm • Sellette 45×45×60 cm

Xira

Table Xira 80×190×72 cm (salle à manger) • 60×60×60 cm • et sur mesures

Kira

Table basse Kira 70×180×40 cm • et sur mesures

Hampi

Les Salons du Palais Royal Shiseido

レ・サロン・デュ・パレロワイヤル・シセイドー
specialty perfume store 香水専門店
142, Galerie de Valois-25, rue de
Valois 75001 Paris
http://www.salons-shiseido.com

A.CD.AD.LD.D:Serge LUTENS

A specialty perfume store that embodies the unwavering sense of beauty of Serge Lutens, the French artist who has been responsible for the creation of the Shiseido image over 20 years. One senses ultimate perfection in the perfumes that are exclusive to the store, the design of the perfume bottles in which they are contained, the magnificent workmanship of the interior décor, and all the various elements that make up the store. The top floor reached by a spiral staircase is in a salon style for a relaxing enjoyment of perfume.

20年間という長きにわたって資生堂のイメージの創造を手がけたフランス人アーティスト、セルジュ・ルタンス氏の確固たる美意識に貫かれた香水専門店。この店限定の香水そのもの、それを収めた香水瓶のデザイン、そして見事な細工に彩られた内装と、ショップを構成する要素のすべてに完成度の高さが感じられる。螺旋階段がいざなう上階は、ゆっくりと香りを愛でるサロンになっている。

Catalog
カタログ

FLEURS D'ORANGER
SERGE LUTENS
SHISEIDO PARIS

UN LYS
SERGE LUTENS
SHISEIDO PARIS

IRIS SILVER MIST
SERGE LUTENS
SHISEIDO PARIS

UN LYS
SERGE LUTENS
SHISEIDO PARIS

Leaflet
リーフレット

Instruction　説明書

Tester
テスター

Perfume Bottle
香水瓶

Angel des Montagnes

AD,CD:Angelique BUISSON

アンジェル・デ・モンターニュ
miscellaneous homeware
インテリア雑貨
90, rue du Bac 75007 Paris
http://www.angeldesmontagnes.com

Tag
商品タグ

Sticker
ステッカー

The maison based in the town of Evian that looks out over the alpine peaks from the shores of Lake Leman now has a shop in Paris. The unique design of the Angel des Montagne product range has a simplicity that fits into contemporary life. It uses a motif of a picture clipping depicting the Pays d'Enhaut area of the Swiss Alps and has a style that communicates the warmth of the handmade.

レマン湖のほとり、アルプスの峰々を望む町、エヴィアンにあるメゾンがパリにオープンさせたショップ。オリジナル商品のデザインは、スイスアルプスの山岳地方「ペイダンオー」に伝わる切り絵のモチーフをアレンジしたものや、手仕事の温かみが感じられるような作風のものなど、素朴なよさはありつつも現代の生活のシーンにもマッチするように考えられており、オリジナリティがある商品が並ぶ。

052

Catalog カタログ

Diptyque

ディプティック
fragrances フレグランス
34, boulevard Saint Germain 75005 Paris
http://www.diptyqueparis.com

A fragrance brand launched in 1961. The Diptyque candles in their various fragrances have in particular been popular for many years. The Diptyque store on Paris's Boulevard Saint Germain, the world centre for international brand goods, features label goods inscribed with black lettering on a white background arranged in an orderly manner in a classical interior décor.

1961年創業のフレグランスのブランド。さまざまな香りのろうそくがとくに有名である。いまや国際的となったブランドのゆりかごともいえるパリのサンジェルマン大通りにあるブティックは、ことのほかクラシックな内装で、ブランドのトレードマークである、白地に黒でデザイン文字が施されたラベルが整然と並んでいる。

Filosofi

A.CD.AD.LD:Lorenz BOEGLI

フィロソフィ
paper products 紙製品
68, rue de Grenelle 75007 Paris
http://www.lorenzboegli.ch

Card Box
カードボックス

Shop Card
ショップカード

With a shop name created from a twist on the spelling of the word "philosophy" but pronounced in the same way, Filosofi's stationery, printed modestly with the shop logo and produced from carefully considered raw materials, and the range of cards that received gold medals in the European Screen Printing Association Competition are hugely popular among people in the know, among them paper connoisseurs, writers, graphic artists, bookbinders and designers, all people who are particular about their paper.

哲学を意味する単語の発音はそのままに、つづりにひとひねり加えた造語がショップネーム。原材料からこだわりをもって製作され、お店のロゴが控えめに印字されたステイショナリー、ヨーロッパのスクリーンプリント協会が主催するコンクールで金賞に輝いたカード類などは、紙にこだわりのある愛好家、作家、グラフィスト、装丁家、デザイナーたちの間ではすでに知名度を得ていて、知る人ぞ知るショップになっている。

j'entrai dans cet état
qui joue sa fin

filosofi

de la poule et de l'oeuf, qui était là en premier?

Letter Set
レターセット

Notebook
ノート

filosofi

et ne croyez pas que nous en sommes restés là:
filosofi culture du papier, 68, rue de Grenelle, 75007 Paris

filosofi

Sticker
ステッカー

filosofi
filosofi
filosofi
filosofi
filosofi
filosofi
filosofi
filosofi
filosofi
filosofi
filosofi
filosofi
filosofi
filosofi
filosofi

Fragonard

フラゴナール
fragrances, miscellaneous goods
香水、雑貨
196, boulevard Saint Germain 75007 Paris
http://www.fragonard.com

A perfumier originally established in the town of Grasse on the Côte d'Azur, known as the town of perfume. In addition to perfume-related products into which Fragonard's skill and knowledge accumulated over many years has been poured, in recent years a range of miscellaneous goods and accessories has been developed to increase the appeal of the range of products available in the store. The products also feature frequently in magazines. The Fragonard packaging also has an established reputation and an endless stream of stylish Parisian ladies frequent the Fragonard store on the Boulevard Saint Germain.

香水の町として知られる、コートダジュールの町、グラースに拠点を置くフレグランスメーカー。長きにわたって培われたノウハウを誇る香り関連の商品に加えて、近年ではオリジナルの雑貨やアクセサリーにも力が注がれ、ショップのラインナップをより魅力的なものにしている。また、デザイン性の高いパッケージングにも定評があることから、ここサンジェルマン大通りに面したショップにも、センスのあるマダムたちの姿が絶えない。

Fleur de vanille — Eau de toilette — 100 ml — 3.3 fl.oz — Fragonard PARFUMEUR

Citron — Eau de toilette — 100 ml — 3.3 fl.oz — Fragonard PARFUMEUR

Figuier fleur — Eau de toilette — 3.3 fl.oz — Fragonard PARFUMEUR

Cerisier en fleurs — Eau de toilette — 100 ml — 3.3 fl.oz — Fragonard PARFUMEUR

Freesia — Eau de toilette — 100 ml — 3.3 fl.oz — Fragonard PARFUMEUR

Lavande — Eau de toilette — 100 ml — 3.3 fl.oz — Fragonard PARFUMEUR

Rose de mai — Eau de toilette — 100 ml — 3.3 fl.oz — Fragonard PARFUMEUR

Verveine — Eau de toilette — 3.3 fl.oz — Fragonard PARFUMEUR

savon à l'huile d'abricot à 3% parfumé à la clémentine

savon à l'huile d'amande douce à 3% parfumé à la rose

savon à l'huile d'olive à 3% parfumé à la lavande

savon à l'huile de pépins de raisin à 3% parfumé à la figue

Fragonard PARFUMEUR à Paris — www.fragonard.com

Fragonard PARFUMEUR à Paris — www.fragonard.com

Six sels de bain parfumés — Six perfumed bath salts — 6 x 30 ml — 6 x 1 fl.oz

Map
地図

Esteban

エステバン

fragrance フレグランス

49, rue de Rennes 75006 Paris
www.esteban.fr

A fragrance brand that originated from the perfume culture of the south of France. Esteban has a comprehensive range of room colognes, from "decorative" colognes that waft from a bottle containing a long, fine bamboo incense stick and fragrances specifically for the bathroom. The brand's image also incorporates a Japanese-style taste that has been realized not only in the design of the packaging, but also in the range of new fragrances.

南仏の香りの文化から発祥したフレグランスブランド。細長い竹ひごを香水瓶に差し込んで、そこから漂う香りを楽しむというしつらえなど、デコレーションとしても楽しめるようなコロンや、バスルームで楽しむ香りなど、ルームコロン系が充実。日本風のテイストをブランドイメージのなかに盛り込んでもいて、パッケージングのデザインはもちろんのこと、新しい香りのたしなみ方の提案でも具体化されている。

FASHION

fashion

fashion

Bonpoint

ボンポワン
children's clothing, miscellaneous
goods, furniture 子供服、雑貨、家具
6, rue de Tournon 75006 Paris
http://www.bonpoint.com

A :François MURACCIOLE   AD:Laure SOLUS BABINET,Pauline JANKOWIAK(assistant)   CD:Christine INNAMORATO
PH(Catalog):Mitty GAIN   PH(Advertising):Arnaud PYVKA   I:SOLEDAD   DF:INTERNAL

Gift Box
ギフトボックス

One of France's best-known children's clothing brands. The sense of style that is typically Parisian is obvious not only in the large number of products on offer but also in the catalogue and invitation cards. The Bonpoint boutique, a magical Bonpoint world, was opened near the Sénat (the upper house of the French Parliament) in a former chateau that surrounds a luxuriantly green courtyard garden. On the basement level is a café where mothers and children can make themselves at home and on the second floor, children's shoes.

フランスを代表する子供服のブランド。パリならではの粋なセンスは、豊富な商品だけではなく、カタログやインヴィテーションカードなど、あらゆるクリエーションの場で発揮されている。リュクサンブール公園のフランス上院のお膝元というロケーションにオープンしたブティックは、昔の邸宅建築を生かし、緑あふれる中庭を囲むようにしながらボンポワンワールドを展開。地下には親子一緒にくつろげるカフェ、2階は靴のスペースになっている。

Invitation Card インビテーションカード

Bonpoint

Catalog
カタログ

Catalog
カタログ

Catalog
カタログ

Invitation Card
インビテーションカード

Bonpoint

Leaflet
リーフレット

Shop Guide 店内案内

New Year Cards
ニューイヤーカードセット

Morganne Bello

A.CD.AD.L:Morganne BELLO

モーガン・ベロ

accessories ジュエリー
66, rue des Saints Pères 75007 Paris
http://www.morannebello.com

Catalog
カタログ

Package
パッケージ

A jewellery brand by Morganne Bello, with stores in Paris and Monaco. She has used numerous elements from nature such as butterflies and flowers as motifs for her creations and has effectively incorporated the motifs into the design of her brand mark and catalogue also. An understated pink, the colour of the brand's image, has been teamed with a chic tone of silver and used in the fabrics for the interior décor.

同名の女性ジュエリーデザイナーによるブランド。パリとモナコに直営店がある。クリエーションのモチーフには、蝶や花などナチュラルなものが多く、ロゴに添えられたマークやカタログのデザインでもそれらが効果的に用いられている。シルバーとコンビネーションされたイメージカラーの落ち着いたピンクは、インテリアのファブリックとしても生かされている。

Chantal Thomass

A:Christian GHION CD:Chantal THOMASS

シャンタル・トーマス
lingerie, miscellaneous goods
ランジェリー
211, rue Saint Honoré 75001 Paris
http://www.chantalthomass.fr

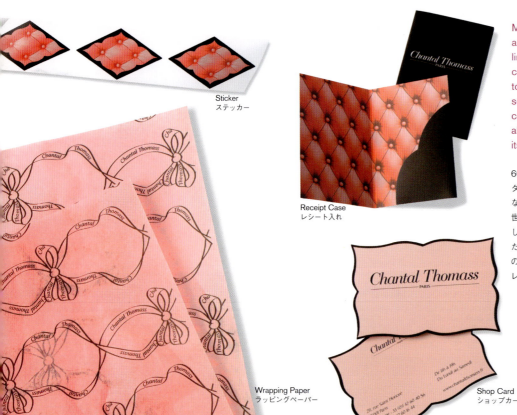

Sticker
ステッカー

Receipt Case
レシート入れ

Wrapping Paper
ラッピングペーパー

Shop Card
ショップカード

Ribbon
リボン

Madame Chantal Thomas who started with pret-a-porter design in the 1960s released a range of lingerie in her 1975 collection that created a storm of controversy at a time when underwear was considered to have only a practical use. The collection that was sensual, luxurious and a little naughty has since then continued to be a favourite among ladies and gentlemen also. The boutique for her brand in Saint Honoré with its pink satin and black lace design is in a salon style.

60年代にプレタポルテデザインを手がけたことから出発したマダム、シャンタル・トーマス。75年にコレクションのショーのなかでランジェリーを発表し、当時は実用一辺倒だった下着の世界に一大旋風を巻き起こした。官能的でラグジュアリー、そして小悪魔的なコレクションは、以来ずっと女性、そして紳士たちをも魅了し続けている。サントノーレのブティックは、このブランドのサロンのようなたたずまい。ピンクサテンと黒いレースがポイントになっている。

Catalog
カタログ

Ovale

A.CD.L:Gilles NEVEU

オーヴァル
children's clothing, miscellaneous goods, accessories 子供服、雑貨、アクセサリー

200, boulevard Saint Germain 75007 Paris
http://www.ovale.com

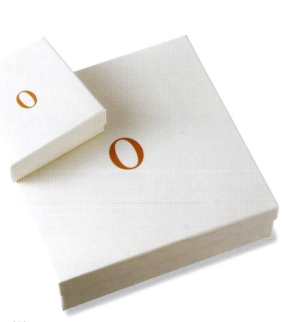

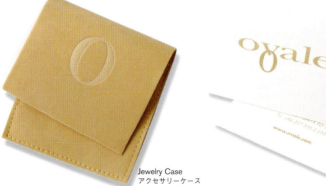

Jewelry Case
アクセサリーケース

Shop Card
ショップカード

Although considered a children's clothing store, the high-quality Ovale brand only sells clothing for newborn babies to one-year olds. It is easy to see the brand's unwavering policy that Ovale range, created by a designer who used to work at Christian Dior, is mostly in ivory to beige tones. The homeware, free from any cuteness, is innovative. The store has been designed to make even men feel comfortable about shopping here.

子供服といっても、生まれてから1歳になるまでの幼児のものだけを扱う高級ブランド。かつてクリスチャン・ディオールで活躍していたデザイナーが手がけるラインナップのほとんどが、アイボリーからベージュまでのトーンで統一されているところにも、確固たるブランドのポリシーがうかがえる。甘さを感じさせない什器類も画期的だが、これは、男性でも居心地の悪さを感じることなくショッピングができるように、という配慮によるもの。

Ovale

Vêtements
Collection de vêtements de 0 à 12 mois unisexe du blanc au beige. Les collections d'été et d'hiver sont présentes toute l'année : lin, coton, laine et cashmere (manteaux, pantalons, brassières, combinaisons et accessoires...)

Infant clothes
Our unique collection offers a complete line of unisex baby clothes from birth to 12 months in whites and beiges. Summer and winter clothes are available all year round in linen, cotton, wool and cashmere (coats, tops and bottoms, undergarments, playsuits and accessories...)

Bijouterie
Grandes et petites médailles en or de toutes les religions. Bracelets et colliers Ovale, la collection cubes...

Jewellery
A selection of large and small gold medals of all faiths. Ovale bracelets and necklaces, our cube collection...

Orfèvrerie
Art de la table en argent massif ou en vermeil (timbales, couverts, ronds de serviette), plusieurs hochets et des curiosités d'Ovale : un écrin à bouchon de champagne, un œuf d'autruche surprenant...

Silverware
Tableware in solid silver or silver gilt (cups, forks and spoons, napkin rings), plus a variety of rattles and curiosities exclusive to Ovale, including a Champagne cork jewel case, a surprising ostrich egg...

Peluches
Notre coup de cœur, le grand ours polaire. Il est dormeur (150cm, 95cm, 65cm) ou assis (100cm, 45cm, 35cm). Des balles bicolores et des doudous.

Paris :
200, boulevard Saint Germain
75007 Paris
Tél +33 (0)1 53 63 31 11

21, rue Marbeuf
75008 Paris
Tél +33 (0)1 47 20 00 42

Robes de Cérémonies
Blanche ou beige, en soie mérinos ou dentelle, tout est possible. Gilles Seran, couturier de la maison, peut imaginer avec vous votre robe « pièce unique », un tendre trésor...

Nos Services
Différents services hors de gammes sont proposés : broderies personnalisées ou toute la collection de vêtements et peluches, gravures sur la bijouterie et l'orfèvrerie. Également livraison à domicile et à l'étranger.

Découvrez un large choix de nos articles à commander sur
www.ovale.com

Discover a w[ ]
items available fo[ ]

Cadeaux de naissance   *Gifts for th[ ]*

Ovale

Message Card メッセージカード

Alain Mikli

A :Philippe STARCK CD,AD,LD:Alain MIKLI

アラン・ミクリ
eyewear 眼鏡
4, rue Bachaumont 75002 Paris
http://www.mikli.com

Post Card
ポストカード

Instruction
説明書

A brand launched by Alain Miki approximately 30 years ago. Alain Mikli is described as a revolutionary of the Parisian eyewear industry for among other things, devising his system where the frame hinges made from a nylon thread can be bent freely inwards and outwards. The design for the recent renovation of the Alain Mikli store in the second arrondissement was by Philippe Starck, a top name of French design. He has created an artistic interior with light playing on the pure white curtains and glass.

アラン・ミクリ氏が30年ほど前にスタートさせたブランド。フレームとつるのちょうつがいの部分が外側にも自由自在に開閉するシステムをあみ出すなど、パリのめがね界の革命児ともいわれている。最近リニューアルした2区の直営店は、フランスのデザイン界の第一人者、フィリップ・スタルク氏によるもの。真っ白なカーテンとガラスに光が戯れる、アーティスティックなインテリアになっている。

Grevi

CD:Roberta and Sylvana GREVI   AD:Giuseppe GREVI

グレヴィ
hats 帽子
1, place Alphonse Deville 75006 Paris
http://www.grevi.com

Catalog
カタログ

Business Card
名刺

Wrapping Paper
ラッピングペーパー

A milliner established in the suburbs of Florence in 1875. The quality of the fashion-forward design and the handiwork has been a favourite of the continually increasing number of Grevi fans around the world and Grevi hats are now sought in department stores and boutiques in main cities around the world. A Grevi store was opened in Florence in 2004 to add to the two here in Paris. The atmosphere created by the antique-style Italian furniture has a modern sophistication at the same time as evoking the elegance of the past.

1875年、フィレンツェ郊外で創業した帽子メーカー。時代の好みをすばやくキャッチしたデザインと手仕事のよさから、愛好家は国境を越えて増え続け、現在では、世界の主だった都市のデパートやセレクトショップなどから求められる商品になっている。直営店としては、2004年にフィレンツェにオープンしたものと、ここパリの2か所のみ。イタリアンアンティークの存在感のある家具がつくる空間は、古きよき、といった趣を残しながらも、現代の洗練が感じられる。

Catalog
カタログ

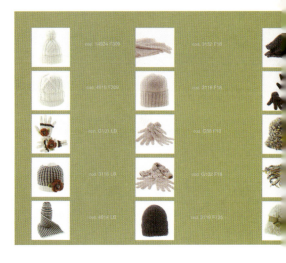

Shop Card　ショップカード

Antoine & Lili

A:Antoine et Lili   CD.D:Martine SENAC

アントワーヌ・エ・リリ
clothing, miscellaneous goods
プレタポルテ、雑貨
3, rue de 29 Juillet 75001 Paris
http://www.antoineetlili.com

Post Card
ポストカード

Tag
商品タグ

A brand that opened a small boutique Montmartre in 1997 and has continued to increase in number, not only in Paris but in other cities of France and also Spain. In addition to the colourful Antoine & Lili clothing that have both an urban and ethnic fashion sense, a range of miscellaneous goods selected with that same sense is also available. The boutiques themselves are colourful and are a charming sight on the streets of Paris.

モンマルトルの坂下に小さなブティックを開いたのが1997年、それから、パリだけでなくフランスのほかの都市やスペインへと直営店を拡大し続けているブランド。都会的ななかにエスニックなテイストをミックスしたカラフルなオリジナルの洋服やアクセサリーのほかに、そのセンスで選んだ雑貨などを扱う。ブティックそのものもカラフルで、パリの町並みのなかの愛らしいアクセントのようになっている。

Paper Bag
紙袋

Lieu Commun

CD,AD,D,DF:Matali CRASSET

リュー・コマン
clothing, miscellaneous goods, CDs
洋服、雑貨、CD
5, rue des Filles du Calvaire 75003 Paris
http://www.lieucommun.fr

lieu commun
tel 01 44 54 08 30
www.lieucommun.fr
mardi - samedi / tuesday - saturday
11h/13h -14h/19h30

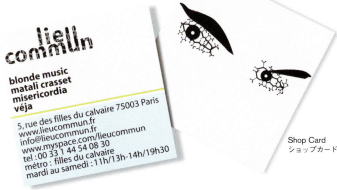

lieu commun

blonde music
matali crasset
misericordia
véja

5, rue des filles du calvaire 75003 Paris
www.lieucommun.fr
info@lieucommun.fr
www.myspace.com/lieucommun
tel : 00 33 1 44 54 08 30
métro : filles du calvaire
mardi au samedi : 11h/13h-14h/19h30

Shop Card
ショップカード

A new concept boutique opened in the north Le Marais district in 2006, featuring products from four types of creators: music produced by Blonde Music, industrial design by matali crasset, clothing by Misericordia and shoes by Veja. Unlike other concept stores and boutiques, the number of lieu commun creators has been limited to four and the store encompasses the totality of their work, including things that are at a trial stage.

北マレ地区に2006年にオープンした、新しいコンセプトのブティック。Blonde Music の編集による音楽、matali crasset によるインダストリアルデザイン、Misericordia の洋服、Veja の靴と、4つの分野のクリエイターの作品を扱う。コンセプトショップやセレクトショップと異なり、クリエイターがこのように少数に限定されており、彼らの仕事を網羅する意味で、試作段階のものも含めた品揃えとなっている。

Ventilo

CD:Arnaud VENTILO

ヴァンティロ
fashion, miscellaneous goods,
café, gallery 衣類、雑貨、カフェ、ギャラリー
27, rue du Louvre 75002 Paris
http://www.ventilo.fr

Event Pamphlet
イベント案内

Catalog
カタログ

A chic, Parisian women's fashion brand featuring sophisticated garments in a range of earthy colours. The entrance to the flagship store in the Rue du Louvre has been turned into a bookstore with books on food, design and travel. In the second-floor gallery, there is a new exhibition of the work of contemporary artists every two months. At the next-door café, you can partake of a meal or a cup of tea in an elegant Asian-inspired atmosphere.

パリのシックな婦人服ブランド。ルーブル通りにあるフラッグショップは、エントランスがライブラリーコーナーになっていて、食やデザイン、旅の本なども扱っている。2階はギャラリーで、コンテンポラリーなアーティストたちの作品を2か月単位で展示。さらにカフェが隣接されていて、アジアのモチーフを取り入れた優雅な雰囲気のなかで、食事とお茶が楽しめる。

Shop Card　ショップカード

Menu　メニュー

Place Mat　ランチョンマット

Bonton/Bonton Bazar

A:François MURACCIOLE CD:Irène COHEN, Eve CAZZANI LD:Sophie CUVELIER
I:SOLEDAD

ボントン／ボントン・バザール

clothing, miscellaneous goods,
furniture 子供服、雑貨、家具
82, rue de Grenelle 75007 Paris/
122, rue du Bac 75007 Paris
http://www.bonton.fr

Sticker
ステッカー

A store that offers children's clothing with that typically Parisian sense of style, a Bonton furniture range and miscellaneous goods, and books. A small cabin has been built in all the Parisian Bonton stores, and animal objets and toys arranged charmingly around the outside. The tasteful Bonton miscellaneous goods such as the mobiles are an object of desire not only for children but for adults also.

いかにもパリらしいしゃれたセンスの子供服をはじめ、オリジナルの家具や雑貨、本などを幅広く扱う店。パリの店舗にはいずれも、キャヴァンヌとよばれる小屋が作られており、その周りに動物のオブジェやおもちゃが添えられていたりして、なんともかわいらしい。また、モビールなどのオリジナル雑貨は、子供だけでなく大人でもほしくなるような、ハイセンスで凝ったつくりのものもある。

PEAPOMOBILE T2
DIVERS
MOBILE APOLLINE

Des Petits Hauts

A,CD,AD,LD:Katia SANCHEZ

デ・プティ・オー
women's fashion 婦人服
5, rue Keller 75011 Paris
http://www.despetitshauts.com

A women's clothing brand that features only tops. This world of poetry and fantasy has established a fan base among young Parisians and the number of Des Petits Hauts stores has steadily increased. The floor that sparkles like candy, the walls covered with British wallpaper and the mix of vintage and modern furniture … the space has been clearly stamped with the store's image.

婦人服、しかもトップスだけにレパートリーを限ったブランド。ポエトリーとファンタジーの世界をミックスしたデザイナーの世界が、若いパリジェンヌたちの支持を得て、着々と店舗を増やし続けている。「キャンディのように」きらきらと光る床、イギリスのウォールペーパーが張られた壁、ヴィンテージとモダンなものとを組み合わせた家具。空間づくりでも、ショップイメージを明確に打ち出している。

Catalog
カタログ

Shop Card
ショップカード

Des Petits Hauts

Tag
商品タグ

Calendar
カレンダー

Colette

CD,AD:SARAH

コレット

boutique コンセプトストア

213, rue Saint Honoré 75001 Paris
http://www.colette.fr

Shop Card
ショップカード

Wrapping
ラッピング

One of the most famous boutiques in Paris. On the first floor are books, CDs, accessories, cosmetics and miscellaneous goods and the second floor is a fashion space. In the basement level is a water bar featuring selected brands of beverages from all over the world and simple meals are available also. The store's trademark blue circles that can be seen throughout the store have been printed on the Colette shopping bags. You won't be able to take your eyes off not only the range of products available but also the store itself.

パリでもっとも有名なセレクトショップのひとつ。1階は本、CD、アクセサリー、コスメティックや雑貨、2階がファッションのスペースになっている。地下は、世界中から銘柄をセレクトしたウォーターバーになっていて、簡単な食事もできる。ショッピングバッグにはトレードマークのブルーの丸。それも微妙にアレンジが加えられたりして、ショップに並ぶアイテムのセレクション以外にも、常に目が離せないショップといえる。

Plastic Bag
ビニール袋

colette

lundi au samedi
11 h à 19 h
–
monday to saturday
11 am to 7pm

COLETTE N°9

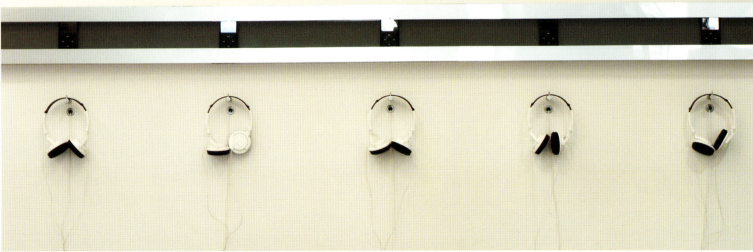

Le Coq Sportif

ル・コック・スポーティフ
sportswear, shoes
スポーツウェア、シューズ
11, rue Tiquetonne 75002 Paris
http://www.lecoqsportif.com

A sportswear brand launched in 1882. In 1948, the bird that is a symbol of France was adopted as the brand's emblem and the brand established an international popularity on sporting occasions such as the Olympics and the football World Cup. The Le Coq Sportif boutique is unique, from the display shelves and grill machines from the butcher shop's inspired by the rooster to the reproductions of the tennis wear worn 25 years ago by the world-title winning French tennis player, Yannick Noah.

1882年生まれのスポーツウェアのブランド。1948年に、フランスを象徴する鳥とされる鶏をエンブレムとして採用し、オリンピックやサッカーワールドカップなどのシーンで国際的な知名度を確立した。ブティックには、テニスの世界タイトルを獲得した仏人プレーヤー、ヤニック・ノア使用モデルの25年目の復刻版などとともに、鶏から発想した、肉屋の陳列台やグリルマシーンによるディスプレイなども見られ、ユニーク。

Shoe Box
シューズボックス

Tag
商品タグ

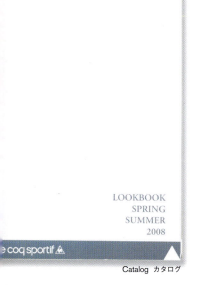

LOOKBOOK
SPRING
SUMMER
2008

Catalog　カタログ

Loft Design By

A,CD,AD,LD:Patrick FRECHE   D:Patrick FRECHE, Delphine BRUNET

ロフト・デザイン・バイ
clothing, miscellaneous goods
洋服、雑貨
56, rue de Rennes 75006 Paris
http://www.loftdesignby.com

Receipt & Shop Card Case
レシート、ショップカード入れ

"Art is a dirty job but somebody's got to do it." … the quote written on the vintage T-shirts seen on the street corners of 1980s New York that has become this brand's slogan. Without overdoing the eccentricity, the tasteful casual wear is arranged around the interior of the store designed to recreate a New York loft with its brick walls, steel-frame pillars and staircases. There are currently three Loft Design By boutiques in Paris and each store has been decorated with tasteful clocks and cash registers.

"art is a dirty job but somebody's got to do it." 80年代のニューヨーク、街角のビンテージTシャツに書かれていたフレーズが、このブランドの格言。奇をてらわず、上質な趣味に裏打ちされたカジュアルウェアが、レンガの壁や鉄骨の柱や階段などで作られたニューヨークのロフトを連想させる店内に並んでいる。ブティックは現在パリには3か所。いずれの店でも、それぞれ味わいのある時計や、レジスターなどがデコレーションされている。

Catalog
カタログ

LOFT
design by...

" *My first Loft* "

Basics
100% EGYPTIAN COTTON

★ NEW-YORK ★

SET OF 3 CREW NECK, SHORT SLEEVE T-SHIRT.
LOT DE 3 T-SHIRT RAS-DU-COU MANCHES COURTES.

NAME : ....

PRODUCED UNDER
THE E AUTHORITY OF THE
LOFT DESIGN BY COMPANY

BABY : 6/12M 18/24M 3/4Y
KIDS : 6Y 8Y 10Y

LOFT
design by...

tailored denim

name : ....

UNDER THE AUTHORITY OF THE LOFT DESIGN BY COMPANY

RHÉTORIQUE
Parisianisme [paRizja´nism], n.m.
Allure, comportement des parisiens.
Ex : LOFT, c'est à deux pas.

Chemise rayée en voile de coton, cravate en tricot, cardigan court
en cashmere et soie et patchs en cuir, jeans slim "nina" noir

28

29

CCES-
OIRES

Chèche en coton double face,
existe en 5 coloris : terre cuite & craie,
gris & bleu, charbon & steel,
indigo & black, steel & terre cuite.

35

42

BABY
& KIDS

Mini dress imprimé et cardigan
en cashmere et soie pochette
en toile imprimée et cuir

095

Marithé+François Girbaud

マリテ・フランソワ・ジルボー
clothing 衣類
7, rue du Cherche Midi 75006 Paris
http://www.girbaud.com

A:Kristian GAVOILLE   CD:Marithé BACHELLERIE, François GIRBAUD   LD:Patrick NORGUET   Wall Decoretion:Patrick BLANC

MARITHÉ
+FRANÇOIS
GIRBAUD®

Shop Card
ショップカード

ouvertures :
lundi 11h - 19h
du mardi au samedi 10h - 19h

Sticker
ステッカー

Shop Card
ショップカード

Tag
商品タグ

A casual wear brand for adults created by the designer couple, Marithe and François Gibaud. They started out making stone-washed jeans and have been pioneers since the 1970s for their development of various types of fabric and three-dimensional cutting. The boutique in Rue du Cherche Midi is groundbreaking with greenery planted on the entire surface of one of the interior walls, an idea that contains this brand's message of sensitivity towards the natural environment.

マリテとフランソワのデザイナーカップルが作り出す、大人のためのカジュアルウェアブランド。ストーンウォッシュによるジーンズの加工に始まり、さまざまな生地の開発や立体裁断など、70年代から常に先駆者的な存在であり続けている。シェルシュ・ミディ通りのブティックは、室内の壁一面にグリーンを植えるという画期的なもので、自然環境のテーマに敏感なブランドのメッセージがこめられている。

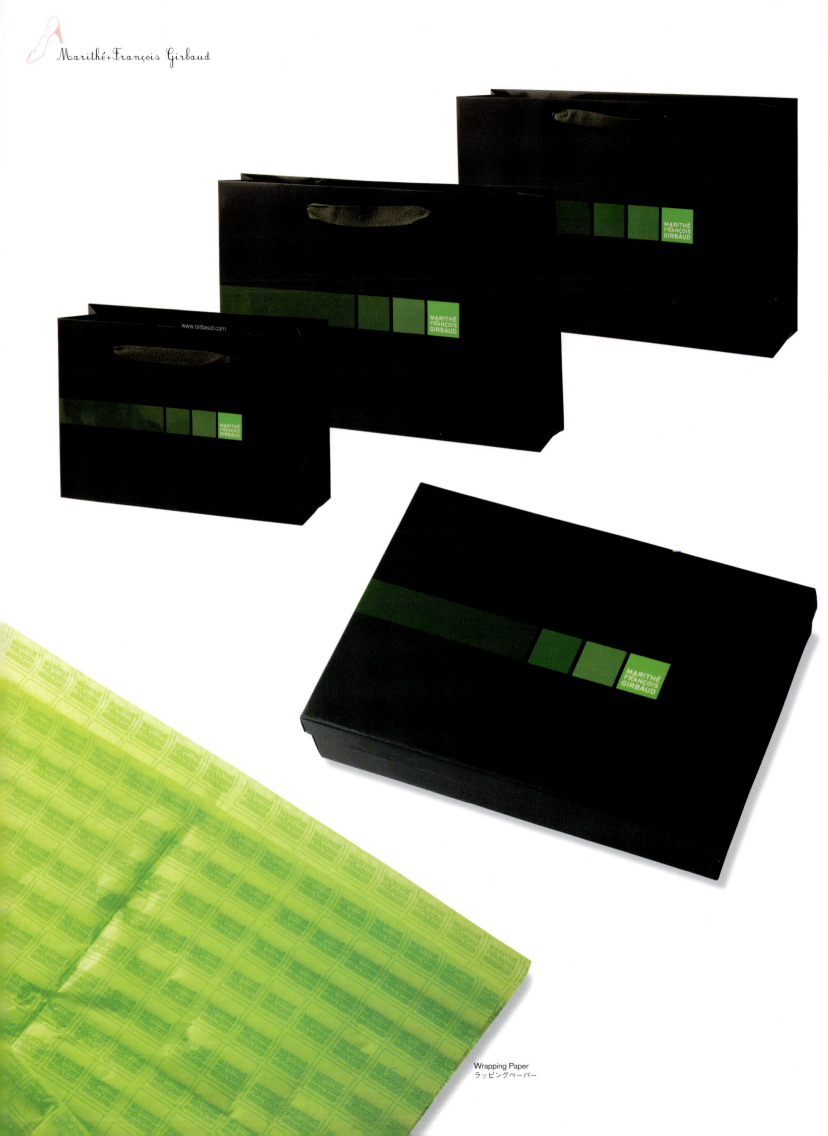

Marithé+François Girbaud

Wrapping Paper
ラッピングペーパー

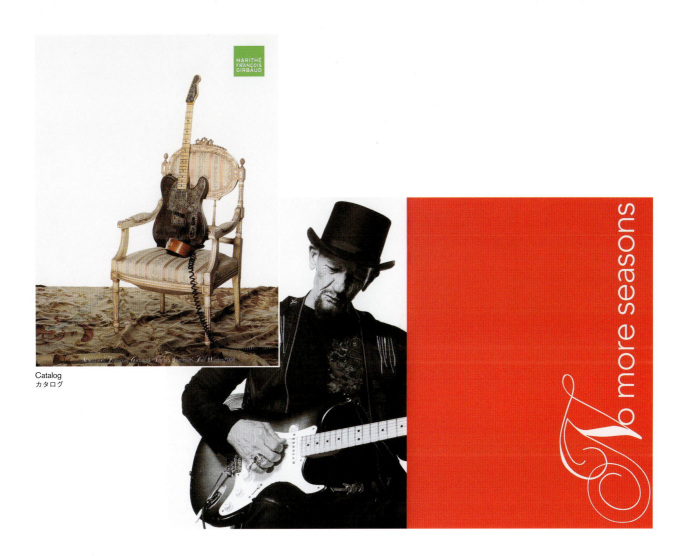

Catalog
カタログ

No more seasons

0₁₂

0₁₃

Lafont

A,CD,LD:Laurence LAFONT   A,D:Thomas LAFONT

ラフォン
eyewear 眼鏡
17, boulevard Raspail 75007 Paris
http://www.lafont.fr

Instruction Case
説明書入れ

Shop Card
ショップカード

An eyewear brand launched by Louis Lafont near the Église de la Madeleine in 1923. Now in 2008, the business has expanded into 38 countries around the world and is still operated by members of the Lafont family. Each of the four Lafont stores in Paris are different including their size, but their window displays have a consistent theme with artistic ideas that harmonize with the Parisian scenery.

1923年にルイ・ラフォン氏がマドレーヌ寺院近くで創業しためがねブランド。2008年現在、世界38か国に販路を広げるほどに成長したが、今もラフォンファミリーによって受け継がれている。パリに4軒ある直営店は、ブティックの広さなどはそれぞれに異なるが、ウィンドーディスプレイには一貫したテーマがあり、パリの景観とよく調和したアーティスティックな趣向が凝らされている。

Shopping Bag
ショッピングバッグ

Greeting Cards
グリーティングカード

FOOD
food
Food

Patrick Roger

パトリック・ロジェ
specialty chocolate store
チョコレート専門店
45, avenue Victor Hugo 75016 Paris
http://www.patrickroger.com

Flyer
フライヤー

Sticker
ステッカー

Shop Card
ショップカード

A boutique belonging to the chocolatier and recipient of a Meilleur Ouvrier de France award, Patrick Roger. He wanted to offer his customers a reminder of nature combined with the sense of luxury of the high-quality chocolates made with carefully selected cacao. He has definitely succeeded with his concept of incorporating nature into an urban space. Each season, he decorates the shop window with elaborate chocolate objets to delight the eyes of passers-by.

M.O.F.（フランス最優秀職人）のタイトルをもつショコラティエ、パトリック・ロジェ氏のブティック。選び抜かれたカカオを用いた高級チョコレートのリュクス感と同時に、彼が打ち出したかったショップイメージは、自然の息吹。生まれ、慣れ親しんできた自然の存在を都会的な空間の中に盛り込むというコンセプトを成功させている。歳時ごとに趣向を凝らしたチョコレートによるオブジェがウィンドーを飾り、道行く人の目も楽しませている。

Package
パッケージ

Shop Card
ショップカード

Catalog
カタログ

Chai 33

A:TANQUEREL

シェ・トロントトワ
café, restaurant, winery
カフェ、レストラン、ワインブティック
Cour Saint-Emilion 75012 Paris
http://www.chai33.com

mars
avril 2008

Flyer フライヤー

Chai 33

Le vin autrement ...

Instruction
説明書

Instruction
説明書

Menu
メニュー

The Saint Emilion district where in olden times the barrels of wine that were shipped up and down the Seine were stored. The street of brick warehouses that has a look from bygone days has been redeveloped as a shopping mall. Chai33 is on the corner of that street. Chai means the cellar in a brewery, a clever name for a multi-use facility incorporating a café and wine shop and which uses the history of the district to good effect. A motif of the triangular roof has also been used in the logo.

その昔、セーヌを船で運ばれてきたワインの樽がここに集積されていたという歴史をもつサンテミリオン地区。往時の面影を今に伝えるレンガ造りの倉庫街は、現在ショッピングモールとして再生している。その一角にあるのがこの店。シェとは、醸造所のカーブという意。土地の記憶を生かした、カフェ、レストラン、ワインショップという複合施設のネーミングとして気が利いている。ロゴにもまた三角屋根のモチーフが使われている。

Chapon

A.CD.LD:Patrice CHAPON

シャポン
specialty chocolate shop
チョコレート専門店
69, rue du Bac 75007 Paris
http://www.chocolat-chapon.com

Catalog
カタログ

Shop Card
ショップカード

Catalog
カタログ

Paper Bag
紙袋

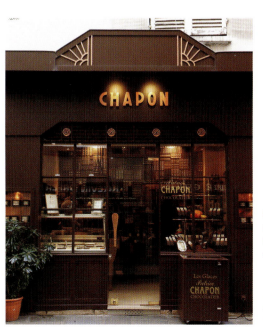

Characters created by the owner based on antique illustrations and advertisements adorn the store's logo, creating nostalgia for what were the good, old days. The molds in which the cake craftsmen used to shape the chocolate in the days of old decorate the walls, along with the lampshades that were converted into copper pots indispensable to the production of jam, to create a unique atmosphere.

ショップのロゴに添えられているのは、アンティークのイラストなどからヒントを得てオーナーが生み出したキャラクター。古きよき時代を思わせるノスタルジックな趣がある。店内の壁には、昔の菓子職人が、チョコレートを成型するのに使っていたという鋳型がびっしりと張りめぐらされ、ジャム作りに欠かせなかったという銅鍋を転用したランプシェードともあいまって、ユニークな雰囲気をかもし出している。

Androuet

アンドゥルエ
specialty cheese store
チーズ専門店
134, rue Mouffetard 75005 Paris
http://www.androuet.com

A specialty cheese store founded in 1909 with six branches in Paris and one in Stockholm, Sweden. As you would expect from a typically Parisian cheese shop, the stock of more than 200 cheeses available naturally includes cheeses produced in France but also in other countries. The cheeses are left to mature in Androuet's cellar and brought out when they are ripe for eating. Androuet's famous clientele has included world-famous stars such as Jean Gabin, Orson Welles and Toshiro Mifune, and the writer, Ernest Hemingway.

1909年創業のチーズ専門店。パリに6店舗のほか、スウェーデンのストックホルムにも店がある。いかにもパリのチーズ屋らしい典型的な造りの店に並ぶのは、フランス産はもちろん、それ以外の国のチーズも含めて200種類以上。自家のカーブで熟成させ、食べごろを見はからって出されるという。歴代の顧客にはジャン・ギャバン、オーソン・ウェルズ、三船敏郎ら世界的なスターや、作家のヘミングウェイも名を連ねている。

Ladurée

A:Roxane RODRIGUEZ

ラデュレ
French patisserie, salon de thé
お菓子、サロンドテ
21, rue Bonaparte 75006 Paris
http://www.laduree.fr

Memo Card
メモカード

Sticker
ステッカー

Ribbon
リボン

Ladurée is arguably the most famous patisserie in Paris in a city brimming over with patisseries. You will find it difficult to choose from the abundant range of cakes and viennoiserie on offer, but the famous macaroons are the reason that Parisians naturally but also people from around the world visit the Ladurée shop. There are several kinds, each with a unique flavour and colour, and new flavours are introduced each season. There is an extensive range of packaging available, and the boxes that are ingeniously redesigned almost every month are used as a beautiful store window decoration.

パリのお菓子屋さんとしてもっとも有名な店のひとつがここ。目移りしそうなケーキやヴィエノワズリーの豊富さもさることながら、パリジャンたちはもちろん世界中からやってくる人々にも人気なのがマカロン。フレーバーは彩りも豊富に10種類ほどあり、季節ごとにニューフェースが加わる。また、パッケージングも充実しており、毎月のように工夫を凝らしたデザインのボックスがお目見えして、ウィンドーを美しく飾っている。

Place Mat
ランチョンマット

Chocolate
チョコレート

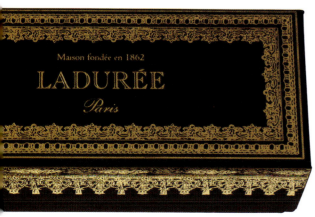

Sugar
砂糖

Paper Bag 紙袋

Le Grand Véfour

A prestigious Parisian restaurant that occupies a corner of the Palais Royal corridor. The original Charles X interior has been designated a Paris landmark. Celebrities of all ages and from all countries who have partaken of the delicacies prepared by a succession of famous chefs are too numerous to mention. Small gold plates engraved with their names have been attached to the restaurant's crimson velvet chairs. A motif of the elegant interior décor can be seen on the menus, the restaurant's business card and the design of the tableware.

パレロワイヤルの回廊の一角を占める、パリでも指折りの高級レストラン。シャルル10世スタイルのインテリアはオリジナルのもので、歴史的建造物に指定されているが、それを舞台に歴代の有名シェフが腕を振るう美食を堪能した古今東西の著名人は、枚挙にいとまがない。深紅のベルベットのシートには、彼らの名前を刻印した小さな金のプレートがはめ込まれている。優美な内装のモチーフは、メニューやショップカード、テーブルウェアのデザインにも見られる。

Instruction
説明書

Menu
メニュー

Shop Card　ショップカード

Oliviers & Co.

オリヴィエ・エ・コー

olive oil store オリーブオイル専門店
128, rue Mouffetard 75005 Paris
http://www.oliviers-co.com

A specialty olive oil store. The design of the retro-style packaging of their products that are already sold throughout the world including France have been updated for a more striking, modern look. There are as many as ten Oliviers & Co stores in Paris, but the Rue Mouffetard store with its olive tree plants and bright atmosphere offers not only oils and various foodstuffs, but also a range of new cosmetic products, and attractive tableware, all making for a fun shopping experience.

オリーブオイルの専門店。フランスをはじめ、すでに世界展開している商品は、レトロな味わいのあるパッケージングから、よりモダンな、くっきりとしたデザインへと衣替えをはかっている。直営店はパリだけでも10軒ほどになるが、ここムフタール通りのブティックには、オイルやさまざまな食品に加えて、新しいコスメティックラインの商品、地中海地方ならではの色と肌合いの食器、さらにはオリーブの鉢植えも置かれ、明るい雰囲気のなかでショッピングが楽しめる。

Invitez la Truffe à votre table !
Quelle soit noire, blanche, d'Italie ou de France.

CONDIMENT BALSAMIQUE BLANC AROMATISÉ À L'ORIGAN
WHITE BALSAMIC CONDIMENT OREGANO FLAVORED

"...OUCHE CRISTALLINE."

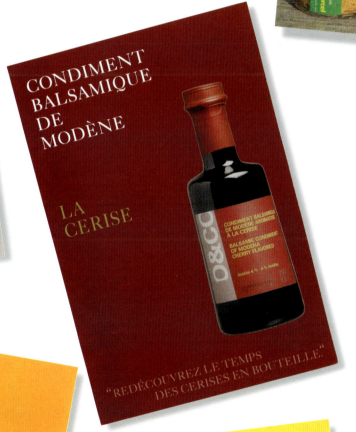

CONDIMENT BALSAMIQUE DE MODÈNE

LA CERISE

"REDÉCOUVREZ LE TEMPS DES CERISES EN BOUTEILLE."

VERONICA ET JOACHIM SANTOS-LIMA
Producteurs

VALE DE LOBOS

Récolte 2007

Région de Ribatejo
Nord de Lisbonne
PORTUGAL

...ECIALITÉ
...ILE D'OLIVE
...RGE EXTRA

...GAMOTE

...Y SIGNÉ OLIVIERS&CO."

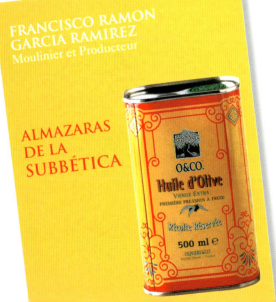

FRANCISCO RAMON GARCIA RAMIREZ
Moulinier et Producteur

ALMAZARAS DE LA SUBBÉTICA

VASSILIOS KOZOBOLIS
Moulinier

MANTINEA
E AVIA

Cojean

A:Hervé VERMESCH

コジャン
restaurant, take-away food
レストラン、テイクアウト
3, place du Louvre 75001 Paris
http://www.cojean.fr

Catalog
カタログ

Event Pamphlet
イベント案内

A new type of store that serves mainly light meals such as sandwiches and salads. It is a similar style to a fast food restaurant, but special care is taken with the ingredients, and fresh produce is offered on a daily basis. The reliefs on the ceiling and walls of the avant-garde yet classic patisserie and the salon de thé in their shop located on the west side of the Musée du Louvre have been used to great effect, painted with the Cojean colour of sky blue to produce a modern atmosphere.

サンドイッチやサラダ、スープといった軽食がメインの、新しいタイプのショップ。ファストフードに類するが、食材へのこだわりはなかなかのもので、常にフレッシュな素材を提供している。ルーブル美術館の東側に位置する店は、前身であるクラシックなパティスリー、サロンドテの天井と壁のレリーフを生かしつつ、イメージカラーのスカイブルー一色に染め上げ、現代的なムードを演出している。

think
pink

body
talk

le jardin
dévasté

hep garçon
un café s'ilvous plaît !

LNHO

07

LNHO

Display Card
ディスプレイカード

nourrir aimer donner

cojean

cojean

cojean

cojean

cojeansugarbabylove

cojeansugarbabylove

cojean

Fauchon

A:Christian BIECHER P:Luc BOEGLY

フォション
foodstuffs, salon de thé
食料品店、サロンドテ
24-26, 30 place de la Madeleine 75008 Paris
http://www.fauchon.fr

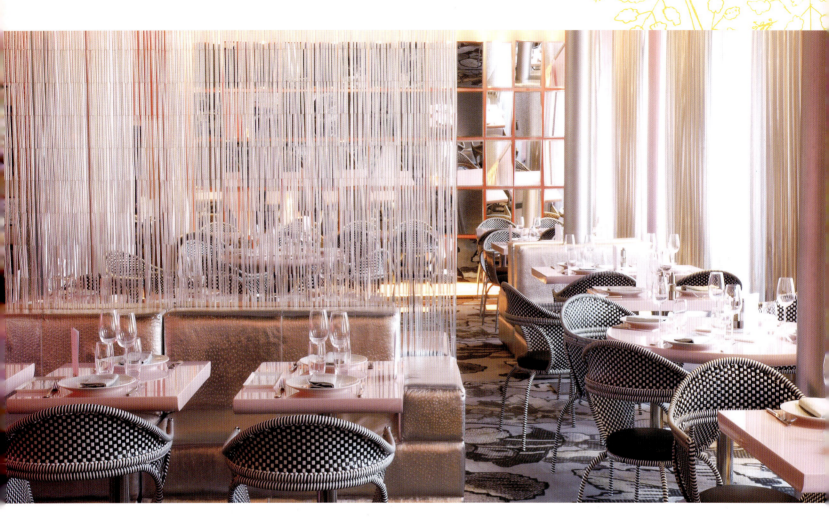

Menu
メニュー

Place Madeleine known for its concentration of high-quality grocery stores. Representative among them is the magnificent Fauchon. The store has undergone a large-scale renovation, and as well as a range of sweet and savoury take-away food, there is also a café and caviar bar in a modern powder pink and silver design offering various styles of epicurean delights.

高級食料品店が軒を連ねることで知られるマドレーヌ広場。そのなかでもひときわ立派な店構えを誇る、代表的な存在がこのショップ。大規模なリニューアルによって生まれ変わったブティックでは、甘辛とりどりのチョイスのテイクアウトができるほか、パウダーピンクとシルバーを基調にしたモダンなデザインのカフェやキャビアバーなども備えており、さまざまなスタイルでの美食の提案をしている。

Senderens

サンドランス
restaurant レストラン
9, place de la Madeleine 75008 Paris
http://www.senderens.fr

A:Noé DUCHAUFOUR LAWRANCE   Lighting Design:Xavier GRUCHET   Motif Design:Yoon HEE AHN

Menu
メニュー

Menu
メニュー

Owner and chef, Alain Senderens, who became a talking point when he relinquished his Michelin star from the days of his Lucas Carton restaurant to follow up the idea of offering to customers the flavours of 3-star quality at a reasonable price. The eponymous restaurant that he subsequently launched abandoned the tablecloths and floral decorations that are an indispensable part of the top-class restaurants for a near future design around the idea of expression with light. In combination with the original art nouveau motif, a fantasy world has been created.

三ツ星クラスの味をリーズナブルな価格で提供したいという思いから、レストラン「ルカ・カルトン」時代の星を"返上"したことで話題になった、オーナーシェフのアラン・サンドランス氏。あらたに自身の名を冠して出発したレストランは、高級店にはつきもののテーブルクロスや花装飾のかわりに、光の表現をふんだんに取り入れた近未来的なデザイン。もともとあったアールヌーヴォーのモチーフとあいまって、幻想的な世界を作り上げている。

Les Ombres

A:Jean NOUVEL

レ・ゾンブル
restaurant レストラン
Musée du Quai Branly 27, quai Branly
75007 Paris
www.lesombres-restaurant.com

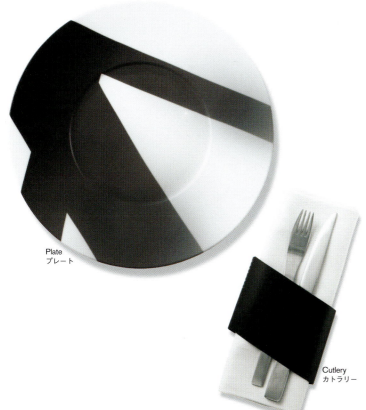

Plate
プレート

Cutlery
カトラリー

Shop Card
ショップカード

LES OMBRES
RESTAURANT

Musée du quai Branly
portail Alma
27 Quai Branly - 75007 PARIS
Tél. 01 47 53 68 00 - Fax 01 47 53 68 18
www.lesombres-restaurant.com

A restaurant on the top floor of the Musée du quai Branly, an art gallery created for exhibiting cultural objects from Asia and the countries of the Pacific. The unique concepts of Jean Nouvel, the popular French contemporary architect who oversaw the design of the entire gallery, are present here also. The play of shadows cast on the floor and the walls by the steel-frame beams that intersect on the glass ceiling is used not only as a feature of the interior design but also in the pattern of the presentation plates. Les Ombres stands for the multitude of shapes of the shadows.

アジア、パシフィックの国々の文物を一堂に展示する場所としてオープンした、ケ・ブランリー美術館の最上階にあるレストラン。館全体を手がけた、現代フランスを代表する建築家、ジャン・ヌーヴェルの独自のコンセプトはここにも生かされている。ガラス張りの天井に交差する鉄骨の梁、それが壁や床に落とす影の戯れは、インテリアデザインだけでなく、プレゼンテーション用の皿の模様としても使われている。レ・ゾンブルとは、影の複数形を意味する。

Richart

リシャール

chocolates チョコレート

258, boulevard Saint Germain 75007 Paris
http://www.chocolats-richart.com

A premier *chocolatier* established in Lyon in 1925. Not only are the chocolates of high quality, passed down through generations, they are perfectly designed, from a colour being assigned to each different flavour, a pattern being drawn on each in various colours, chocolate boxes that resemble a chest of drawers, and tubes of cream-filled chocolates that are not only delicious but also visually appealing.

1925年、フランスのリヨンで創業した高級チョコレート店。代々引き継いできたクオリティの高さに加えて、デザインも充実。フレーバーごとに色分けし、それぞれの色でチョコレートの表面に模様を描いたり、引き出し状になった箱に引き手をつけたりといった工夫のほか、クリーム状のチョコレートが入ったチューブタイプのものなど、舌だけでなく、目にもうれしい心配りがなされている。

Richart

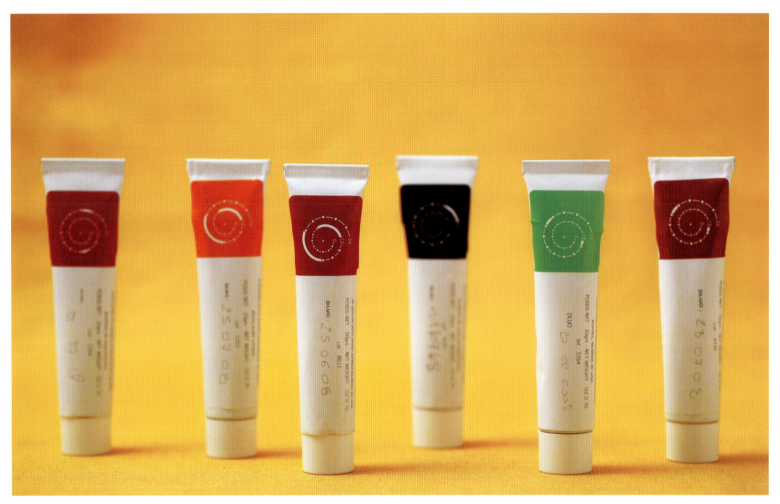

Les Petits RICHART

Collection "phare" de la Maison RICHART, elle s'adresse à toutes celles et tous ceux qui aiment voyager, découvrir de nouveaux horizons,... en un mot sortir des sentiers battus.

Avec les Petits RICHART, découvrez les arômes du cacao de Madagascar, ou de Papouasie en ganache; surprenez-vous en découvrant les parfums d'un praliné pur pistache de Sicile ... Laissez-vous envoûter par la douceur du Néroli, la fraîcheur du basilic ou de la cardamome; laissez-vous séduire par le parfum capiteux de la lavande, du thym ou du curry...

Allégé en sucre et en matières grasses pour ne garder que l'essentiel, chacun de ces chocolats ne pèse que 4 grammes : un bijou qui ne se partage pas !

[www.RICHART-chocolats.com]

Bienvenue à la Maison de la Dégustation®

Célébrer

Mariage, naissance, baptême, anniversaire,... autant d'occasions de célébrer avec sa famille, ses amis, un événement marquant de notre vie.

Chocolats personnalisés

Ronds ou carrés ? Ganache, praliné ou coulis ?
Pour des chocolats uniques, nous mettons notre richesse gustative et notre savoir-faire à votre disposition.
N'hésitez pas à nous soumettre vos rêves...

Je t'aime

Une collection de chocolats aux formes suggestives et aux intérieurs mêlant douceur, tendresse, pour lui dire tout votre amour en toute occasion !

Les Dragées

À événements extraordinaires... collection de dragées extraordinaires !

Laissez-vous séduire par la dragée amande "Avola" de Sicile sélectionnée par Michel RICHART.
Sa silhouette élégante, sa saveur intense, sa délicate amertume se marient à merveille à une fine coquille juste sucrée et délicatement parfumée à la vanille naturelle.

Amateurs de douceur ? Retrouvez toute la finesse et la puissance aromatique d'un chocolat noir du Venezuela dosé à 70% de cacao pur (recette RICHART), dans un large choix de coloris ou enveloppé dans une véritable feuille d'argent.

Alliant tradition et modernité, les pochons et tiroirs blancs mettent en valeur les dragées, telles des pierres précieuses dans leur écrin.

Catalog
カタログ

[www.RICHART-chocolats.com]

133

Le Boulanger des Invalides

CD:Philippe JOCTEUR

ル・ブーランジェ・デ・ザンヴァリッド
bakery パン、お菓子
14, avenue de Villars 75007 Paris

14, avenue de Villars - angle rue d'Estrées - 75007 Paris
Tél : 01 45 51 33 33   Mº St François Xavier

A bakery in a corner of a quiet residential area in the south of Invalides. The ceiling of the shop is adorned with a magnificent painting that you might expect to see in a French chateau or art gallery and the same tiles have decorated the walls of the building since 1881. Before being taken over in 2006 by Monsieur Jocteur who built a proud career over 20 years in Lyon, the bakery that stood here was expanded, a salon de thé added, and the bakery redesigned so that customers were able to see the bakers at work.

アンヴァリッドの南、閑静な住宅地の一角にあるパン屋さん。アイボリー色の調度で統一された店内で天井に目をやれば、そこにはシャトーか美術館にでもあるような見事な絵が描かれており、壁のタイルともども1881年からその建物を飾っているものという。リヨンですでに20年のキャリアを誇ったジョクター氏が2006年に譲りうける前にも、ここはパン屋さんだったが、拡張して、サロンドテ部分と、実際にパンを作っている職人さんの仕事風景も眺められるようになっている。

Ducs de Gascogne

デュック・ドゥ・ガスコーニュ
foodstuffs 食料品
18, rue Vignon 75009 Paris
http://www.ducsdegascogne.com

A grocery store named after the Dukes of Gascony, a district in the south west of France. In addition to its major product of *foie gras*, a special product of Gascogne, Ducs de Gascogne also offers products that we associate with the bountiful farmland of France, including pork and gibier pâté. Counter seats have been set up along the window of the shop and snacks including sandwiches using Ducs de Gascogne ingredients are served to the workers in nearby office buildings.

フランス南西部の地方、ガスコーニュの公爵たちというネーミングの食料品店。その地方の特産であるフィアグラをメインに、豚やジビエのパテなど、いかにもフランスの恵み豊かなテロワール（大地）を連想させる食品を扱っている。付近はオフィス街ということもあり、店のウィンドー沿いにはカウンター席が設けられ、このマークの食材を使ったサンドイッチなどの軽食のサービスもしている。

137

Boutique Maille

ブティック・マイユ
mustard, grocery store
マスタード、食材
6, place de la Madeleine 75008 Paris
http://www.maille.com

Depuis 1747
BOUTIQUES MAILLE
6 place de la Madeleine - PARIS
32 rue de la Liberté - DIJON

Instruction
説明書

A long-established store that sells mustard, a famous product of the Bourgogne district. The brand's products are already famous all over the world, but there are only two Maille stores, one in Dijon and the other in Place Madeleine in Paris. The store's interior with rows of mustards and vinegars of every kind, including the fresh mustard that is available only from the store and poured into specially made pots in a similar way to draft beer, is an impressive sight. There are mustard containers with hand-drawn designs available.

ブルゴーニュ地方の名物として知られるマスタードの老舗。このマークの製品はすでに世界中で有名だが、直営店はディジョンとここ、パリのマドレーヌ広場の2か所。ショップのみで手に入る、生ビールのような要領で特製のつぼに注がれるフレッシュマスタードをはじめ、あらゆる種類のマスタードやビネガーが並ぶ店内は壮観。手描きの模様が施されたマスタード容器なども揃っている。

Boutique Maille

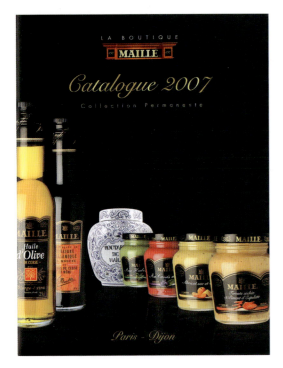

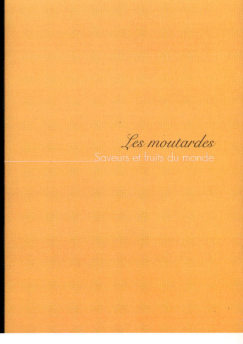

Les moutardes
Saveurs et fruits du monde

Moutarde Maille
Abricot sec et Curry

Les moutardes
Caractères et Terroirs

Girolles, échalotte et cerfeuil
Chanterelles with shallots and Chervil
La chasse aux saveurs est ouverte :
toutes les viandes, les belles volailles
et le gibier sont à l'honneur.

Au Bleu
Blue Cheese
Son caractère vigoureux fait merveille
sur les viandes rouges.

Verjus et Miel*
Verjuice and Honey
Une alliance douce-acide sur viandes
blanches et rouges, une pointe de mystère
dans la vinaigrette.

Noisette et Muscade
Hazelnut and Nutmeg
L'une sent bon la forêt, l'autre a un parfum
de soleil. À deux, elles enchantent les
viandes et les salades d'hiver.

Au miel et Fruits confits
Honey and Preserved Fruit
Reine des viandes et surtout du gibier,
son charme opère en jouant des contrastes.

Aux Noix
Walnut
Une noix de moutarde aux noix sur la noix
de jambon, le compte est bon !

Au Cassis de Dijon
Dijon blackcurrant
À faire voyager avec les belles viandes
et poissons grillés des barbecues d'été.

Au Marc de Bourgogne*
Marc de Bourgogne
Seule escorte digne des fromages
de caractère, et du gibier naturellement...

Au Cognac*
Cognac
Pourquoi faire flamber les viandes rouges
quand la moutarde s'en charge ?

15

Les vinaigres
13 vinaigres aux arômes fruités et a

Vinaigre Balsamique
à l'écorce d'Orange amère

20

Les vinaigres

Vinaigre de Xérès* à l'origan
Oregano Sherry
Son goût corsé et subtil et sa belle couleur
brune font merveille sur les poissons,
les crustacés et les salades créatives.

Vinaigre de Xérès*
à la tomate séchée
Sun dried Tomato Sherry
Un à-coût de soleil supplémentaire,
en dégustation sur les viandes blanches
comme le rôti de porc, et en marinade
avant tout barbecue.

Vinaigre balsamique de Modène
au jus de cerise et mûre

Vinaigre de vin blanc* à la truffe
White wine with truffle
Un arôme subtil de truffe noire pour relever
celui de tous les mets délicats : le foie gras,
les salades gourmandes, les crustacés
et les petits légumes de printemps.

Vinaigre de vin blanc*
au citron et à l'aneth
White wine with lemon and dill
Une recette aux accents nordiques, à jouer
sur les poissons, et dans les salades à base
de céréales (taboulé, boulghour...) sans
oublier les lentilles.

Vinaigre de vin blanc* au zeste
et jus de pamplemousse
White wine with grapefruit

140

Unico

ユニコ
restaurant レストラン
15, rue Paul Bert 75011 Paris
www.resto-unico.com

A:Joulia MARCELO CD:Alexis CLADIERE LD:Rosaura LORENZO

Menu
メニュー

Shop Card
ショップカード

A restaurant specializing in Argentinean cuisine, with Argentine beef at the top of the menu. A traditional butcher's shop that in previous years were seen everywhere in Paris was renovated with a mix of '70s-style design that is obvious from the wallpaper, and traditional French *boucherie*, to create a truly unique décor. The space that was allocated for the women's toilets used to be a cold-store room where you can imagine the pieces of meat hanging from the hooks. The heavy doors and the knob that you have to grasp firmly to open and close the door have been retained, making a visit to the toilets a memorable experience.

アルゼンチンビーフを筆頭に、アルゼンチン料理を得意とするレストラン。以前はパリのどこにでもあったような、トラディショナルな肉屋の店舗を改装したもので、壁紙に象徴されるような70年代風のテイストが、かつての肉屋のイメージと渾然一体となって、ユニークなデコレーションになっている。化粧室になっている場所は、昔は肉の塊がぶら下がっていたであろう冷蔵室。分厚い扉、しっかりと握って開閉するノブなどはそのままで、空間としての面白みがある。

Kong

A:Philippe STARCK LD:Thibaut MATTHIEU P:Patricia BELAIR I:Thibault de CATHEU

コング
restaurant レストラン
1, rue du Pont Neuf 75001 Paris
http://www.kong.fr

Kong's avant-garde design by Philippe Starck was the talk of the town at the time of its opening. With its perfect location overlooking the Seine, the interior of Kong that occupies the top floor of a building at the foot of Pont Neuf creates a sense of being inside a glass capsule that reaches into the sky. A feature throughout the décor is the placement of elements that we associate with contemporary Japan such as manga and characters.

フィリップ・スタルクの手による前衛的なデザインがオープン当時話題をさらったレストラン。ポンヌフのたもとのビルの最上階の先端、空に張り出したガラスのカプセルのなかにいるような感覚を与える店内からは、セーヌ河を眼下に見下ろせる、という絶好のロケーションにある。インテリアデコレーションの随所に、マンガやキャラクターものなど、現代の日本を連想させる要素を配しているのも特徴的。

KONG®
BAR RESTAURANT

1, rue du Pont Neuf
75001 Paris
Tel : 01 40 390 900 Fax : 01 40 390 910
http://www.kong.fr

BAR RESTAURANT
KONG®

KONG ! HAPPY PARTY IN PARIS
le dancefloor mixé et revisité par Béatrice Ardisson
PARIS PREMIERE

ASSIETTES
KONG®

KONG®

CHAMPAGNE / 10 cl.

COUPE MOET		13 €
COUPE MOET ROSE		15 €

CHAMPAGNE AOC /

MOET & CHANDON	Brut Imperial	120 €
MOET & CHANDON ROSE	Brut Imperial	125 €
VEUVE CLIQUOT	Brut	130 €
VEUVE CLIQUOT ROSE	Millesimé	135 €
RUINART ROSE	Brut	140 €
DOM PERIGNON	Millesimé	230 €
KRUG GRANDE CUVEE	Brut	260 €
CRISTAL ROEDERER	Brut	280 €
MOET & CHANDON	Brut Imperial (Magnum)	230 €
VEUVE CLIQUOT	Brut (Magnum)	250 €

BOUTEILLE / 180 € TOUTE BOUTEILLE PRISE EST CONSOMMEE LE SOIR MEME

WHISKY	Jack Daniel's, J.Walker Black, Chivas
VODKA	Belvédère
GIN	Bombay, Tanqueray

VERRE / 13 €

WHISKY / 4 CL. J&B, J.Walker Red

VODKA / 4CL. Absolut blue, Absolut citron, Smirnoff

GIN / 4CL. Gordon's

RHUM / 4CL. Bacardi carta blanca

TEQUILA / 4CL. Tequila Jose Cuervo Especial

LIQUEURS / 4CL. Amaretto di saronno, Baileys original irish cream, Pimm's, Fernet Branca, Get 27, Grand Marnier, Kahlua, Limoncello, Manzana verde, Marie Brizard, Sambuca

SANS ALC

HA LONG
DETENTI

SHORT /

CAIPIRIN
CAIPIRO
MOJITO

MEDIUM

COSMOP
APPLE M

LONG / 1

LONG IS
SEX ON
TEQUILA
TOM CO

CHAMPA

BELLINI
ROSSELI

BIERES /

SOFTS /
oranguin
orange, p

Foucher

フーシェ
chocolates, specialty tea store
チョコレート、お菓子
30, avenue de l'Opéra 75002
http://www.chocolat-foucher.fr

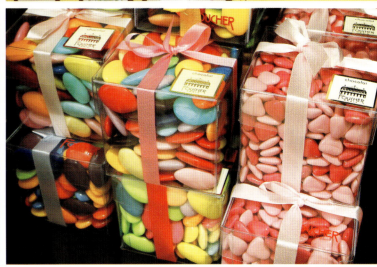

A long-established chocolate and cake store at the centre of Avenue de l'Opéra that extends in a straight line from Opéra to the Musée du Louvre. Passers-by stop here naturally for the extensive range of sweet delights, but first and foremost to see the boxes displayed in the shop window that are reproductions of what is now a large collection of the packaging created for Foucher by illustrators for more than one hundred years.

オペラ座からルーブル美術館へと一直線に伸びるオペラ大通りのなかほどにある、チョコレートとお菓子の老舗。豊富なスイーツのバリエーションはもちろんのこと、まずはウィンドーに飾られた箱のデザインに、通りを行く人が足をとめる。それらの意匠は、1世紀ほどにわたって、その時代ごとに活躍したイラストレーターたちがこの店のために作成したパッケージングの復刻版で、一大コレクションといえるほどの蓄積があるという。

Shop Card, Business Card
ショップカードと名刺

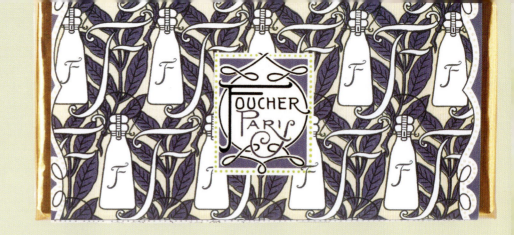

Foucher

PLAQUETTE AU CAFÉ
FOUCHER PARIS

Côte d'Ivoire

Depuis 1819

FOUCHER
PARIS

30, avenue de l'Opéra

Chocolat au lait avec 40% de cacao

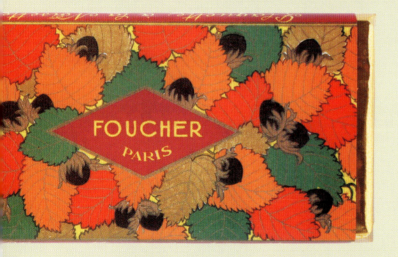

FOUCHER
PARIS

PLAQUETTE FON
Foucher-Pari

PLAQUETTE à L'ORANGE
FOUCHER PARIS

Verlet

A:François MURACCIOLE I:WOZNIAK

ヴェルレ
coffee, specialty tea store, café
コーヒー、紅茶専門店、カフェ
256, rue Saint Honoré 75001 Paris
http://www.cafesverlet.com

Sticker
ステッカー

Rue Saint Honoré in Paris is famous for being tightly packed with stores selling brand goods, but amongst them is a place where time appears to have stood still. Regular customers quietly read their newspapers and savour the fragrant coffee in an atmosphere where you can forget the noisy hustle and bustle of the world outside. Verlet was upgraded in 2005 but the original 1920s furniture has been retained to create an atmosphere of the days of old.

パリのサントノーレ通りといえば、ブランドショップがひしめく通りとして有名だが、そんななかにあって、ここはまるで時がとまったかのようなたたずまい。常連たちが新聞を広げながらしずかに、香り高いコーヒーを味わっている様子は、表の喧騒をしばし忘れさせてくれるような別世界である。2005年にリニューアルしているが、1920年代から使われてきた家具はそのままに、かつての趣を最大限に生かしている。

Lavinia

A:Antonio de la PEÑA

ラヴィニア
wine, liquor ワイン、洋酒
3, boulevard de la Madeleine 75001 Paris
http://www.lavinia.com

au prix du magasin.   Every wine that we serve has the same price as

Catalog
カタログ

With a store interior of 1,200 square metres in total and three floors, Lavinia could be described as a department store for liquor. A range of 6,000 products is available, including 3000 brands of wines from all over France and 200 from 30 countries around the world and other products such as cognacs and brandies. There is a 130-seat restaurant on the top floor of the store where the walls are decorated with the original wine-related illustrations produced for the cover of the Lavinia annual catalogue.

総面積1200㎡、3フロアをゆうゆうと使った店内は、まさにお酒のデパート。扱うワインは、フランス各地から3000銘柄、世界30か国から2000銘柄と幅広く、さらにコニャックやブランデーなどのお酒も合わせると、トータルで6000種の規模を誇る。店内上階には130席のレストランもあり、その壁には、毎年のカタログの表紙のために描かれた、ワインにまつわる絵の原画が飾られている。

Kusmi Tea

A.CD:Sylvain OREBI AD:Joana ZARAKARIASA

クスミティー
specialist tea store, salon de thé
紅茶専門店、サロンドテ
56, rue de Seine 75006 Paris
http://www.kusmitea.com

Established in St. Petersburg in 1867 by Pavel Michailovitch Kousmichoff. The family subsequently relocated to Paris via London and Berlin more than a century ago. The design of its packaging has changed slightly over time but basically the same motif has been used consistently since the business was started. Kusmi's vinyl shopping bags are of a novel design. The Kusmi store in the Saint Germain district has a minimalist décor and is bursting with light. On the second floor, you can partake of a cup of tea or a snack.

1867年にロシア人、クスミコフ氏がサンクトペテルブルグで創業。一家はロンドン、ベルリンを経てパリに拠点を構え、すでに1世紀以上がたつ。パッケージデザインは時代とともに多少の変化が加えられているが、基本的には創業以来一貫したモチーフを使用。ビニール製のショッピングバッグなどはより斬新なイメージを打ち出している。サンジェルマンデプレ地区にできた直営店は、光あふれるクリーンな印象で、2階では、お茶と軽食が楽しめる。

PARIS 1917 : au moment où la révolution tonne en Russie, la famille
et installe ses ateliers au 75 avenue Niel dans le 17ème. L'adresse
se plonger dans l'ambiance début 20ème que l'on y retrouve. BEF

Shop Card
ショップカード

Place Mat
ランチョンマット

Catalog
カタログ

Novelty
ノベルティ

Culture Bière

A:DRAGON ROUGE ARCHI

キュルチュール・ビエール
bar, restaurant
バー、ブティック、レストラン
65, avenue des Champs Elysées 75008 Paris
http://www.culturebiere.com

A store dealing in beers, located at the centre of the Champs-Élysées. At the entrance there is a counter where you can rest your feet weary from walking around the city and enjoy Culture Bière's original brew. In an adjacent shop, there is a range of beers as well as ingredients for making the establishment's beer. The second floor has a restaurant, and there is a spacious beer bar in the basement for you to make yourself at home in.

シャンゼリゼ通りのなかほどに位置するビールにまつわる店。エントランスには町歩きの疲れを気軽に癒やせるようなカウンターがあり、この店オリジナルのビールも楽しめる。隣接するショップには、各種のビールのほかに、ショップオリジナルのビールの原料にちなんだ食材や、関連のグッズも充実。さらに2階はレストラン、地下には広々としたビールバーがあり、思い思いの形でくつろげる空間が融合している。

Jour

AF:PRAVDAARKITECT CD,LD:ALIOCHA

ジュール
fast food
ファストフードレストラン、サラダバー
29, rue du Louvre 75002 Paris
http://www.jour.fr

A departure from the concept of the heavy French lunch, that also fits into our modern urban lifestyle. Enjoy light lunches including salads that you put together yourself in the minimalist interior or as a take-away. Jour means "day." The concept of spending each day in an upbeat mood can be seen in the bright green used for the packaging and also in the façade and chairs on the terrace.

胃に重たい料理ではなく、現代の都会のライフスタイルに合ったランチを、というコンセプトから出発。その場で組み合わせて選べるサラダなどの軽食は、クリーンな店内、あるいはテイクアウトで味わうことができる。ジュールとは、日、一日という意味合い。日々新鮮な気分で、というような意図は、パッケージングをはじめ、店のファサードやテラスの椅子にも使われているグリーンの明るさからも感じられる。

Shop Card
ショップカード

158

Mariage Frères

CD,AD,D:Franck DESAINS

マリアージュ・フレール
teas, salon de thé
紅茶専門店、サロンドテ
13, rue des Grands Augustins 75006 Paris
http://www.mariagefreres.com

A world-famous specialty tea store. The Mariage Frères packaging with a yellow logo on a black background is a familiar sight in France, but it is the packaging used for the release of new tea flavours and seasonal products that becomes a regular topic of conversation. In the boutique on the Left Bank close to Saint Germain, large tins of tea are arranged along one wall to make a spectacular sight. The salon de thé on the upper level has a colonial-style décor and offers teas and snacks.

世界的に有名な紅茶の専門店。黒地に黄色のマークのパッケージングはすでにおなじみだが、新しいフレーバーや、季節限定商品の発表のたびに、その新鮮なパッケージングもまた話題になる。サンジェルマンにほど近い、左岸のブティックでは、はかり売りのお茶が入った大ぶりの缶が壁一面に並び、壮観。上階がサロンドテになっていて、コロニアルスタイルのインテリアのなかで、お茶はもちろん食事も楽しめる。

Sushi Shop

A:Miguel CANCIO MARTIN   AD,LD:Nicolas MATERNIK

スシショップ
sushi restaurant and take-away
レストラン、テイクアウト、宅配
178, rue de Courcelles 75017 Paris
http://www.sushishop.fr

The Japanese food boom of the past few years has firmly taken hold in Paris and sushi is now a popular choice. Sushi shops set up by French people have sprung up one after another in Paris, offering take-away sushi and a delivery service. The most prominent of all the sushi shops is this chain. Its shops with their stylishly coloured packaging and interior have been opened mainly in upper-class residential areas and business districts.

数年来の和食ブームはパリにすっかり定着し、スシはいまやポピュラーな食の選択肢。本家本元の日本人によるものではないスシ店が、続々と誕生し、ファストフード、デリバリーといった手軽な楽しみ方を斬新なデザインとともに提案している。なかでももっとも勢いのあるのがこのチェーン。シックな色合いを基調としたパッケージングやインテリアによるショップを、高級住宅地やオフィス街を中心に展開させている。

Menu
メニュー

SUSHI**SHOP**

SUSHI**SHOP**

SUSHI**SHOP**

JAPANESE FUSION FOOD

JAPANESE FUSION FOOD

JAPANESE FUSION FOOD

créations

SUSHIS (2 pièces)
Yellow tail	5.00
Spicy salmon (saumon, sauce spicy, piment japonais)	4.00
Spicy tuna (thon, sauce spicy, piment japonais)	4.50

SPRING ROLLS (6 pièces)
Ebi fry (tempura de crevettes, avocat, sauce curry)	6.00
Chili crab (char de crabe spicy, avocat, menthe)	6.00
Crispy duck (canard laqué, concombre, oignon vert, sauce hoisin)	6.00
Tuscan (crevette, pignons, mesclun, mayonnaise à l'huile de truffe blanche)	7.00

CALIFORNIA (6 pièces)
Ebi fry (tempura de crevettes, avocat, sauce curry)	6.00

CHIRASHI MARINÉ (15 pièces)	16.00
Thon, saumon, poireau, concombre, coriandre, sauce vinaigrée	

⑥ PIÈCES soya rolls
riz et poisson cru
enroulés dans
une feuille de soya

Soya rolls
Saumon Avocat	5.00
Saumon Cheese	5.00
Avocat Cheese	5.00
Concombre Cheese	5.00
Thon Avocat	5.00
Thon cuit Avocat	5.00
Chicken Avocat	5.00

Spicy sushis

new collection

spring & rainbow rolls

california & big rolls

makis & temakis

sushis & sashimis

menus midi

compositions

boissons, desserts

Albert Ménès

Package Design:Agence MÉDIANE

アルベール・メネス
foodstuffs 食料品
41, boulevard Malesherbes 75008 Paris
http://www.albertmenes.fr

Ribbon
リボン

Shop Card
ショップカード

Shop Card
ショップカード

A grocer offering a wide range of traditional French flavours including jams, biscuits, fish, tinned soup, and rare bottled vegetables. The products, each with their own special packaging, are seen not only in France but also in smart grocery stores in other countries, and are also popular as gifts, but this is the only Albert Ménès store. As well as the Albert Ménès brand products, well-known regional cakes are also available.

ジャム、ビスケット、魚やスープの缶詰、珍しい野菜の瓶詰など、幅広いレパートリーでフランスの伝統の味を提供している食品メーカー。それぞれに趣向が凝らされたデザインのパッケージは、フランス国内はもちろんのこと、海外の気の利いた食料品店でもお目にかかることができ、プレゼントとしても人気だが、ショップとしてはここが唯一の存在。マークの商品に加えて、地方の名物菓子なども揃う。

Poissonnerie du Dôme

ポワッソヌリー・デュ・ドーム
fresh fish shop 鮮魚
4, rue Delambre 75014 Paris
http://www.poissonneriedudome.com

A:SLAVIK

Langoustines

POISSONNERIE
LANGOUSTES VIVANTES

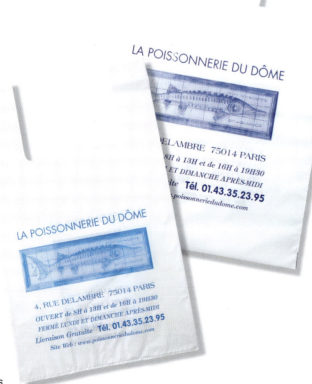

LA POISSONNERIE DU DÔME

4, RUE DELAMBRE 75014 PARIS
OUVERT de 8H à 13H et de 16H à 19H30
FERMÉ LUNDI ET DIMANCHE APRÈS-MIDI
Livraison Gratuite   Tél. 01.43.35.23.95
Site Web : www.poissonneriedudome.com

LA POISSONNERIE DU DÔME

LA POISSONNERIE DU DÔME

Shop Card
ショップカード

A neighborhood of Vavin, Montparnasse was a former gathering place for Paris-based artists such as Picasso and Tsuguharu Fujita, and used to be described as a "crossroads of the world." Poissonnerie du Dôme is a fresh fish shop located in a side street. There are many who claim that the quality of the fish is the highest in Paris. It not only serves fish connoisseurs but also has many famous restaurants among its clientele. The coloured illustrated tiles that are reminiscent of Japanese fish prints charmingly decorate the exterior and along the top of the interior walls is artwork in a fish motif.

ピカソや藤田嗣治ら「パリ派」の画家たちが集い、その時代には「世界の交差点」とも評された、モンパルナスはヴァヴァン界隈。その路地を入ったところにある鮮魚店。そのクオリティはパリで一番との呼び声も高く、食通の人々をはじめ、多くの有名レストランもこの店の顧客である。魚拓を連想させるような色絵タイルがその外観を魅力的なものにし、店内の壁の上部にも魚をモチーフにしたアートが施されている。

Hôtel du Petit Moulin

A,AD,LD,D:Christian LACROIX P,I:Christophe BIELSA

オテル・デュ・プティ・ムーラン
Hotel ホテル
29/31, rue de Poitou 75003 Paris
http://www.hoteldupetitmoulin.com

Letterhead
レターヘッド

Shop Card
ショップカード

Memopads
メモパッド

Christian Lacroix, one of the top designers of our time, oversaw the renovation of Hotel du Petit Moulin. With a different décor for each of the 17 rooms of the hotel, the dream from his childhood of inhabiting a different interior every day has been realized. The top-notch composition of his unrestrained imagination including Venetian-style ornamentation and British colour schemes has been carried throughout the hotel. On the exterior, the façade of the oldest bakery in Paris has been preserved, giving the hotel an even more unique story.

手がけたのは当代ファッションデザイン界の第一人者、クリスチャン・ラクロワ氏。毎日違うインテリアに暮らすという、幼いころの彼の夢を実現させたかのように、全17室のインテリアはまったく雰囲気の違うもの。ベネチア風の装飾、英国風の色彩など、彼一流の、自在な発想のコンポジションがホテル全体に行き渡っている。外観はパリでもっとも古いパン屋さんの部類に入るもので、その遺構を残したことでもまた、場所の独自性を物語っている。

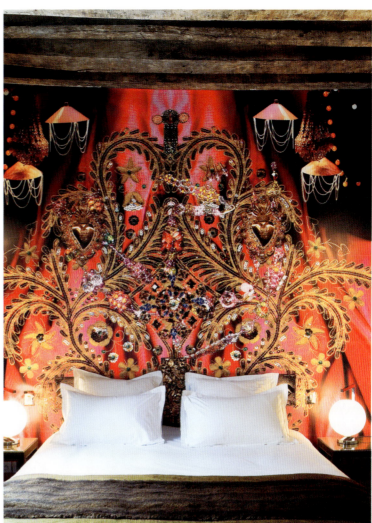

Leaflet
リーフレット

Catalog
カタログ

Door Hangers
ドアハンガー

David Sauvage By Massato

ダヴィッド・ソヴァージュ・バイ・マサト
hair salon 美容室
9, rue de Luynes 75007 Paris

A:Regis DALLIER CD:David SAUVAGE

Shop Card
ショップカード

A hair salon in a small side street off Boulevard Saint Germain, formerly a branch of the famous Salon Massato that is now run by David Sauvage. Massato's logo that consists of letters of the alphabet arranged into a picture of a face can be seen on the salon's business card and hair care products. The interior colour scheme in white, black and red matches the towels, walls and acrylics.

サンジェルマン大通りから、小道をすこし入ったところにあるヘアサロン。ダヴィッド・ソヴァージュ氏が、有名サロンMASSATOの支店だった店を引き継いだもので、ショップカードやヘアケア製品に、アルファベットをアレンジして顔をあらわした、MASSATOのロゴマークが見える。インテリアの配色は、白、黒、赤。それらが、タイル、壁布、アクリルなど、さまざまなマチエールで組み合わされている。

Hôtel Sezz

Decorator: Christophe PILLET

オテル・セーズ
hotel ホテル
6, avenue Frémiet 75016 Paris
http://www.hotelsezz.com

Key Case
キーケース

Letterhead
レターヘッド

sezz
6, avenue Frémiet - 75016 PARIS
Tel : +33 (0)1 56 75 26 26 - Fax : +33 (0)1 56 75 26 16
mail@hotelsezz.com - www.hotelsezz.com

Shop Card
ショップカード

Hotel Sezz is hidden away in a small side street not far from the Eiffel Tower in Passy, a quiet upper-class residential area in the 16th arrondissement. Beyond the elegant and classically Parisian brick façade, the interior opens out into a modern design space. The traditional hotel reception area has been cleverly done away with and the hotel entrance converted into a relaxed salon-style area.

閑静な高級住宅地として知られる16区はパッシー地区。エッフェル塔からそう遠くない小道に、隠れ家のように存在するホテル。いかにもパリらしい、クラシックで優雅な石造りのファサードの内側には、モダンなデザイン空間が広がっている。レセプションを取り払って、エントランスそのものがすでにサロンのような、くつろいだ雰囲気になっているのも、思い切ったコンセプトのひとつ。

Catalog
カタログ

jeu des lumières

let there be light

www.mazzega.com

AVMazzega

Coaster コースター

Dental Kit
歯磨きセット

Comb くし

Sewing Kit ソーイングセット

Luggage Number
荷物札

Anne Fontaine Spa

アンヌ・フォンテーヌ・スパ
spa facility スパ
370, rue Saint Honoré 75001 Paris
http://www.annefontaine.com

A:Andrée PUTMAN P:Satoru UMETSU

Catalog
カタログ

The fame of the Anne Fontaine "white blouse" brand has expanded internationally. She has set up her first Anne Fontaine brand spa in the basement of her new boutique in Rue Saint Honoré. The spa was designed by Andrée Putman in a soft, white colour that captures the brand's essential image, to create a space of transparent purity and chic tranquility. The image has been incorporated also into the packaging of an oil and cream product range.

白いブラウスのブランドとして国際的に名声を広めたアンヌ・フォンテーヌ。サントノレ通りの新ブティックでは、地下にこのブランドとしては最初のスパを開設した。デザインは、アンドレ・プットマン女史によるもので、本来のブランドイメージにも通じる柔らかみのある白がテーマカラーとなって、透明感さえ感じさせるピュアな面持ちとシックな落ち着きをあわせもつ空間になっている。オイルやクリームなどのパッケージもまたそのイメージの延長にある。

Hôtel Lumen

LD,D,DF:Claudio COLUCCI A:Alain DARONIAN

オテル・リュメン
hotel ホテル
15, rue des Pyramides 75001 Paris
http://www.hotel-lumenparis.com

Key Case
キーケース

Letterhead
レターヘッド

Room Directory

HOTEL LUMEN

Paris Louvre

Instruction
説明書

Mini Bar

HOTEL LUMEN

Paris Louvre

Menu
メニュー

A 32-room boutique hotel located on Rue des Pyramides close to the Musée du Louvre. Walk across the threshold of the hotel, leave the hustle and bustle of the street outside behind and enter a different world. The guest rooms on the Saint Roch side of the hotel have special views that are a well-kept secret place in the middle of the big city. The motif that is teamed with the hotel's logo is a chandelier and a carpet.

ルーブル美術館にほど近い、ピラミッド通りに位置するブティックホテル。全32室。にぎやかな通りから一歩なかに足を踏み入れれば、表の喧騒からまったく隔離されたかのように、空気感が変わる。サンロック教会側の客室からは、都会の真ん中の秘密の場所のような、とっておきの風景が望める。ロゴとともにあらわされているモチーフは、シャンデリアやじゅうたんなどにも、それぞれアレンジした形で使われている。

Letterhead レターヘッド

La Maison Rouge

ラ・メゾン・ルージュ
contemporary art foundation
コンテンポラリーアート財団
10, boulevard de la Bastille 75012 Paris
http://www.lamaisonrouge.org

A:Jean-Yves CLEMENT   AD:Paula AISEMBERG   LD:Jocelyne FRACHEBOUD

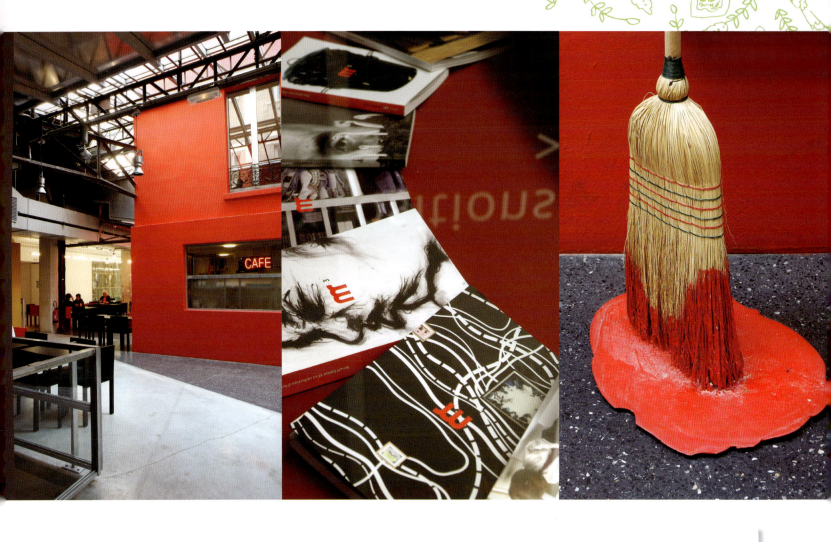

Admission Ticket
入場券

Shop Card ショップカード

Letterhead レターヘッド

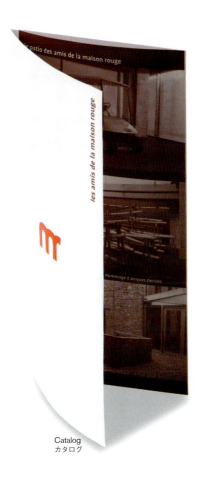

Catalog
カタログ

Catalog
カタログ

A private foundation that holds regular exhibitions of contemporary art. What was originally a factory and a surrounding group of dwellings on the banks of a canal close to Bastille occupying 2,000 square metres underwent a major renovation to be converted into an art gallery comprising four exhibition spaces and a café. For a witty touch, the walls of the entranceway and passages have been painted red to tie in with the name, Maison Rouge, and a small objets attached to the locker keys.

コンテンポラリーアートの企画展を定期的に行っているAntoine de GALBERT氏の財団。バスティーユに近い運河沿い、昔は工場と、それを取り囲む住宅群だったという2000㎡の規模を、4つの展示室とカフェを備えた施設として大改装している。「赤い家」というネーミングにちなんで、エントランスや通路の壁を赤で統一しているほか、ロッカーキーにも小さなオブジェをあしらうなど、ウィットが利いたデザインとなっている。

Catalog
カタログ

Londres, 2001, extrait de la vidéo

pilar albarracín
mortal cadencia

Née à Seville, capitale de l'Andalousie, où elle a vécu et étudié, Pilar Albarracín (1968) a fait de ses racines andalouses le terrain d'exploration de son art. Dans ses photographies, dessins, broderies, sculptures, installations, vidéos ou performances, elle explore l'intérieur et déconstruit par la parodie, l'ironie, l'excès ou l'humour, les images de l'«espagnolité», cette construction d'une identité commune de la grande nation espagnole instrumentalisée par Franco (1939-1975). Plus de trente ans après la mort du dictateur, les éléments du folklore andalou vampirisés par le franquisme continuent de symboliser

Voyageurs du Monde

ヴォワイヤジャー・デュ・モンド

travel agency トラベルショップ

55, rue Sainte Anne 75002 Paris
http://www.vdm.com

Bookmark
しおり

Sticker
ステッカー

A travel agency offering customized travel experiences. The agency has been divided into sections corresponding to world travel destinations and each section decorated with objets from that locality. A map of the sky has been drawn on a wall that extends across three floors to encourage a desire to travel in the agency's customers. Voyageurs du Monde also has Paris' best bookstore for travel books and a boutique store offering products imported from countries around the world.

カスタムメイドの旅の提案をするトラベルエージェンシー。店内では、世界の行き先の地域別にセクションが分かれ、それぞれに、その土地の文物を取り入れたデコレーションをしている。3フロアにわたって一面に広がる壁には、空の地図が描かれていて、旅心を誘う演出になっている。旅行関連のものとしては、パリ最大級の書店と、世界中の国々から集められた品々を販売するブティックも併設している。

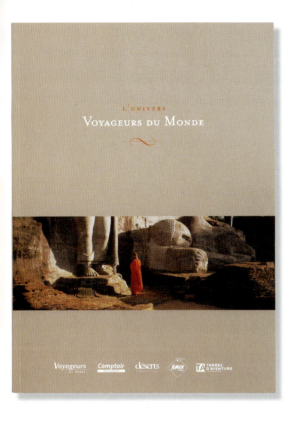

L'UNIVERS
VOYAGEURS DU MONDE

Voyageurs · Comptoir · déserts · · TERRES D'AVENTURE

Voyages en individuel · Séjours · Voyages sur mesure

VOYAGEURS EN
GRÈCE ET EN CROATIE

Athènes · Crète · Îles Grecques · Croatie · Îles Croates · Monténégro

Voyageurs
DU MONDE

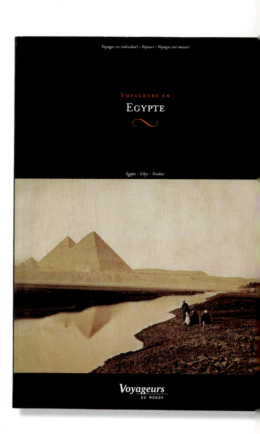

Voyages en individuel · Séjours · Voyages sur mesure

VOYAGEURS EN
EGYPTE

Egypte · Libye · Soudan

Voyageurs
DU MONDE

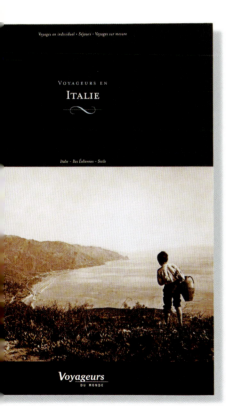

Voyages en individuel · Séjours · Voyages sur mesure

VOYAGEURS EN
ITALIE

Italie · Îles Éoliennes · Sicile

Voyageurs
DU MONDE

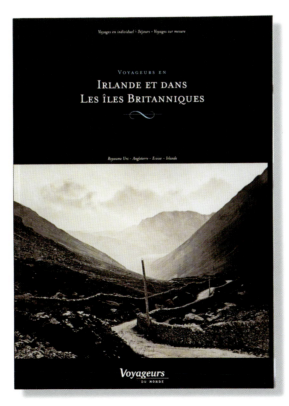

Voyages en individuel · Séjours · Voyages sur mesure

VOYAGEURS EN
IRLANDE ET DANS
LES ÎLES BRITANNIQUES

Royaume Uni · Angleterre · Écosse · Irlande

Voyageurs
DU MONDE

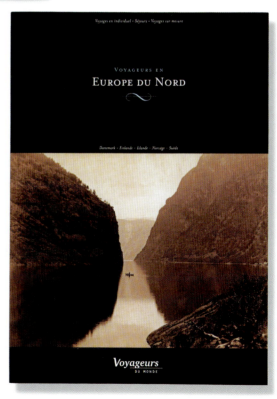

Voyages en individuel · Séjours · Voyages sur mesure

VOYAGEURS EN
EUROPE DU NORD

Danemark · Finlande · Islande · Norvège · Suède

Voyageurs
DU MONDE

Les Bains du Marais

レ・バン・デュ・マレ
spa facility ハマム、サウナ
31-33, rue des Blancs Manteaux 75004 Paris
http://www.lesbainsdumarais.com

CD,A:Eric BENITAH

Leaflet リーフレット

A spa facility that incorporates a hamman, a sauna, a beauty treatment and hair salon. The marble and sandstone hamman and the lustrous mahogany décor of the impressive entrance to the salon and restaurant may be in the heart of Paris, but Les Bains du Marai is where you can experience a North African maghreb place of healing. The emblem on the front door and the packaging of the Les Bains du Marais product range are in an oriental style also.

ハマム、サウナ、エステティックサロン、理髪室などが一体になった施設。大理石と砂岩とから成るハマム、つややかなマホガニーの調度が印象的なエントランスやレストランコーナーなど、パリの都心にいながらにして、モロッコやチュニジアといったマグレブ諸国の癒しの場に身をゆだねることができる。入り口の扉やオリジナル製品のパッケージに見られるエンブレムもまたオリエンタル。

Point WC

ポワン・ヴェー・セー
public toilet 公衆トイレ
26, avenue des Champs Elysées 75008 Paris
http://www.pointwc.com

A,CD,LD:Nina VIRUS

A "top-quality" public toilet opened on the Champs-Élysées. The toilet stalls that come in a variety of sizes and styles from one that fits you and your children to another with an ethnic décor could be described as a kind of showroom for the toilet, where the toilets can actually be used and offer a unique toilet-going experience. In terms of design, Point WC has progressed from the idea of the toilet being merely a box-shaped room, to incorporating advanced functions that includes self-cleaning after each use. At the Point WC Shop, a range of goods such as toilet paper and brushes, also with a smart design, are available for purchase.

シャンゼリゼ通りにオープンした"高級公衆トイレ"。子供と一緒に入れるもの、エスニック調など、それぞれにスタイルの異なるブースは、使用可能なトイレのショールームといえる。デザイン的な箱というハード面だけではなく、1回ごとにお掃除されるというソフトの面でも、かつて例をみないハイクラスのサービスが提供される。ショップコーナーでは、トイレットペーパーやブラシなど、こだわりのデザイングッズも販売している。

Shop Card, Sticker
ショップカードとステッカー

Point Card　ポイントカード

Press Release
プレスリリース

Shop Card
ショップカード

Cordonnerie Vaneau

The street corners of Paris are even today dotted with shoe repair shops where you can catch sight of craftsmen at work, and the name Cordonnerie Vaneau has almost become a brand name of the shoe repair industry. In the Rue Vaneau shop that has existed since 1946, the walls are chock full of photographs of famous people from various walks of life who have been customers of Cordonnerie Vaneau for decades. There are now stylish Cordonnerie Vaneau corners inside department stores with an atmosphere only found in a shop that specializes in manual work and that even dares to use old-fashioned brown paper bags.

職人の仕事風景が見えるような靴の修理店は、パリの街角にいまでもちらほらと点在するが、ここはいわばその業界のブランド的存在。1946年からあるというヴァノー通りの店には、各界の有名人の写真がびっしりと貼られ、彼らが古くからの顧客であることがわかる。現在では、デパートの中にもしゃれたコーナーがあるほどだが、あえて昔ながらのクラフト紙の袋を使っているあたりに、手仕事の店ならではの味がある。

Index

Submittors

Submittors

IN-STORE DISPLAY GRAPHICS
店頭コミュニケーショングラフィックス

Page: 216 (Full Color)　¥14,000+Tax

店頭でのプロモーション展開においては、空間デザインだけでなくグラフィックデザインが果たす役割も重要です。本書では、空間のイメージとグラフィックツールのコンセプトが一貫している作品をはじめ、限られたスペースで有効活用的なディスプレーキットや、P.O.P. の役割も果たすショップツールなどを広く紹介します。

A useful display tool for a limited space, display examples which show the harmonization among packaging, shop interior and in-store promotional graphics, a creative point-of-sale tool which stands out among others. This book is a perfect resource for designers and marketing professionals.

995

CHARACTER DESIGN TODAY
キャラクターデザイン・トゥデイ

Page: 232 (Full Color)　¥14,000 + Tax

キャラクターは企業と消費者とを結ぶ有効なコミュニケーションツールといえます。競合商品との差別化をはかるため、企業のサービスを消費者にわかりやすく伝えるためなど、その役割は様々です。本書では、キャラクターのデザインコンセプト、プロフィールとともに広告やツールの展開例を収録。巻頭では、キャラクターが決定するまでの過程やボツ案を特集し、長く愛されるキャラクターをデザインするポイントを探ります。

200 successful characters with each profile, concept as well as the graphic examples. A featured article about the process of creating a character from scratch is also included with useful examples.

984

NEO JAPANESQUE GRAPHICS
ネオ ジャパネスクグラフィックス

Page: 208 (Full Color)　¥14,000 + Tax

近年、さまざまなデザイン作品のなかに、伝統的な和風意匠から脱却し、より現代的に洗練され、アレンジされた新しい和テイストのデザインが数多く見られるようになりました。本書は、広告・装幀・パッケージなどのカテゴリごとに、各分野の優れた"新・和風デザイン"を紹介します。次世代の和風デザインが集結した見ごたえのある１冊として、あらゆるクリエイターにお薦めします。

This collection presents a tremendous array of the next generation Japanese-style design that is currently drawn attention in creative circles as expressed in the form of flyers, catalogs, posters, packaging, CD jackets, calendars, book design, and more.

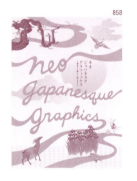
858

PACKAGE FORM AND DESIGN
ペーパーパッケージデザイン大全集　作例＆展開図（CD-ROM 付）

Page: 240 (Full Color)　¥7,800+Tax

大好評の折り方シリーズ第３弾。製品を守りブランドアイデンティティーのアピールとなるパッケージ。本書ではバラエティーに富んだかたちのペーパーパッケージ約200点を国内外から集め、その作例と展開図を紹介していきます。展開図を掲載した CD-ROM 付きでクリエイターやパッケージ制作に関わる人たちの参考資料として永久保存版の１冊です。

This is the third title focusing on paper packaging in "Encyclopedia of Paper Folding Design" series. The 150 high quality works are all created by the industry professionals; the perfect shapes and beautiful designs are practical and yet artistic. The template files in pdf file on CD-ROM.

941

GIRLY GRAPHICS
ガーリー グラフィックス

Page: 200 (Full Color)　¥9,800 + Tax

"ガーリー"とは女の子らしさの見直しや、ポップでありながらもキュートといった、女の子らしさを楽しむポジティブな姿勢を意味します。そんな"ガーリー"な空気感を、ポスター・DM・カタログ・パッケージなどのデザイン領域で、魅力的に表現した作品を紹介します。

A word "girly" represents an expression of reconstructing positive images about being girls. Today, those powerful and contagious "girly" images with great impact successfully grab attentions not only from girls but also from a broad range of audience. This book features about those 300 enchanted and fascinated advertisements such as posters, catalogs, shop cards, business cards, books, CD jackets, greeting cards, letterheads, product packages and more.

1009

NEO JAPANESQUE DESIGN
ネオ ジャパネスク デザイン

Page: 224 (Full Color)　¥14,000+Tax

2006 年 2 月に発刊し好評を得た「ネオ ジャパネスク グラフィックス」。待望の第二弾「ネオ ジャパネスク デザイン」がいよいよ登場。ショップイメージ・ロゴ＆マークのカテゴリが新たに加わり、内容・クオリティともにバージョンアップした"和"デザインの最前線を紹介します。

This is the sister edition to "Neo Japanesque Graphics" published in 2006, and this new book includes even more modern yet Japanese taste designs which will give creative professionals inspirational ideas for their projects. Among various graphic works, this second title features shop design such as restaurants, bars and hotels, also features a variety of Japanese logos.

996

文字を読ませる広告デザイン 2

Page: 192 (Full Color)　¥9,800 + Tax

パッと見た時に文字が目に入ってきて、しかも読みやすいデザインの広告物やパッケージの特集です。優れたデザインや文字組み、コピーによって見る側に文字・文章を読ませることを第一に考えられた広告を厳選します。ポスター、新聞広告、チラシ、車内吊り、雑誌広告、DM、カタログ、パンフレット、本の装丁、パッケージ、看板・サインなど多岐なジャンルにわたり紹介します。

Sales in Japan only.

934

NEW ENCYCLOPEDIA OF PAPER-FOLDING DESIGNS
折り方大全集　カタログ・DM 編（CD-ROM 付）

Page: 240 (160 in Color)　¥7,800+Tax

デザインの表現方法の１つとして使われている『折り』。日頃何げなく目にしている DM やカード、企業のプロモーション用カタログなど身近なデザイン中に表現されている『折り』から、たたむ機能やせり出す、たわめる機能まで、約200点の作品を展開図で示し、『折り』を効果的に生かした実際の作品を掲載していきます。

More than 200 examples of direct mail, cards, and other familiar printed materials featuring simple / multiple folds, folding up, and insertion shown as they are effected by folding along with flat diagrams of their prefolded forms. With CD-ROM.

490

DESIGN IDEAS FOR RENEWAL
再生グラフィックス

Page: 240 (Full Color)　¥14,000 + Tax

本書では "再生" をキーワードにデザインの力で既存の商業地や施設、ブランドを甦らせた事例を特集します。リニューアル後のグラフィックツールを中心に、デザインコンセプトや再生後の効果についても紹介します。企業や地域の魅力を再活性化させるためにデザインが果たした役割を実感できる1冊です。

A collection of case studies - with "regeneration" and "renewal" as their keywords - showing commercial districts, facilities and brands brought back to life through the power of design. Focusing on mainly the post-renovation graphic tools, we present the design concepts and their regenerative effects through which readers will see the role that design can play in reigniting the allure of companies and communities.

977

GRAPHIC SIMPLICITY
シンプル グラフィックス

Page: 248 (Full Color)　¥14,000 + Tax

上質でシンプルなデザイン —— 見た目がすっきりとして美しいのはもちろんのこと、シンプルなのに個性的な作品、カラフルなのに上品な作品、フォントやロゴがさりげなく効いている作品など、その洗練されたデザインは見る人を魅了してやみません。本書は厳選された作品を国内外から集め、落ち着いた大人の雰囲気にまとめ上げた本物志向のグラフィックコレクションです。

Simple, high-quality design work: not just crisply elegant and eye catching, but uncluttered yet distinctive, colorful yet refined, making subtly effective use of fonts and logos; in short, sophisticated design that seduces all who sees it.

973

1&2 COLOR EDITORIAL DESIGN
1・2色でみせるエディトリアルデザイン

Page: 160 (Full Color)　¥7,800+Tax

少ない色数でエディトリアルデザインする際には、写真の表現や本文使用色に制限がある分、レイアウトや使用する紙に工夫や表現力が問われます。本書は1色、2色で魅力的にレイアウトされた作品を、インクや用紙データのスペックと併せて紹介します。

This book presents many of well-selected editorial design examples, featuring unique and outstanding works using one or two colors. All works in this single volume present designers enormous hints for effective and unique techniques with information on specs of inks and papers. Examples include PR pamphlets, magazines, catalogs, company brochures, and books.

956

PICTGRAM & ICON GRAPHICS 2
ピクトグラム＆アイコングラフィックス 2

Page: 208 (Full Color)　¥13,000 + Tax

本書では、視覚化に成功した国内・海外のピクトグラムとアイコンを紹介します。空港・鉄道・病院・デパート・動物園といった施設の案内サインとして使用されているピクトグラムやマップ・フロアガイドをはじめ、雑誌やカタログの中で使用されているアイコンなど、身近なグラフィックまでを業種別に掲載。巻末に、一般的によく使われるピクトグラム（トイレ・エスカレーター・駐車場など）の種類別一覧表を収録。

Second volume of the best-seller title "Pictogram and Icon Graphics". Full-loaded with the latest pictograms around the world. Signage, floor guides and maps in airport, railway, hospital, department store, zoo and many more. Contained a wide variety of icons, including those found in catalogs and magazines, etc.

935

FASHION BRAND GRAPHICS
ファッション グラフィックス

Page: 160 (Full Color)　¥7,800 + Tax

本書は、ファッション、アパレルにおけるグラフィックデザインに力を入れた販促ツールを、厳選して紹介します。通常のショップツールはもちろん、シーズンごと、キャンペーンごとのツールも掲載。激しく移り変わるファッション業界において、お客様を飽きさせない、華やかで魅力的な作品を凝縮した1冊です。

The fashion brands that appear in this collection are among the most highly regarded in Japan and herein we introduce some of their commonly used marketing tools including catalogues, shopping cards and shopping bags, together with their seasonal promotional tools and novelties. This publication serves for not only graphic designers, but also people in the fashion industry, marketing professionals.

962

BEST FLYER 365DAYS NEWSPAPER INSERT EDITION
ベストチラシ 365 デイズ　折込チラシ編

Page: 256 (Full Color)　¥14,000 + Tax

一番身近な広告媒体である新聞の折込チラシ。地域に密着したお得な情報を提供するものから、セレブ＆クールで夢のようなビジュアルのものまで多種多様です。本書では、1年間（365日）の各セールスシーズンでまとめたものから、1枚だけで効果的に商品をPRしたチラシまで、優れたデザインの旬な折込チラシ800点を収録しています。広告の制作に携わる人びとに必携のデザインサンプル集です。

This book contains many examples of excellently designed, topical flyers, ranging from seasonal advertisements to flyers for a single product. It is an anthology of design samples for creative professionals in the advertising industry.

936

BEYOND ADVERTISING: COMMUNICATION DESIGN
コミュニケーション デザイン

Page: 224 (Full Color)　¥15,000+Tax

限られた予算のなか、ターゲットへ確実に届く、費用対効果の高い広告をどのように実現するか？ 今デザイナーには、広告デザインだけでなく、コミュニケーション方法までもデザインすることが求められています。本書では「消費者との新しいコミュニケーションのカタチ」をテーマに実施されたキャンペーンの事例を幅広く紹介。様々なキャンペーンを通して、コミュニケーションを成功させるヒントを探求します。

Reaching the target market a limited budget: how is cost effective promotion achieved? What are the most effective ways to combine print and digital media? What expression reaches the target market? The answers lie in this book, with "new ways and forms of communicating with the consumer" as its concept.

948

WORLD CALENDAR DESIGN
ワールドカレンダーデザイン

Page: 224 (Full Color)　¥9,800+Tax

本書では国内外のクリエーターから集めたカレンダーを特集します。優れたグラフィックスが楽しめるスタンダードなタイプから、形状のユニークなもの、仕掛けのあるものなど、形状別にカテゴリーに分けて紹介します。カレンダー制作のデザインソースとしてはもちろん、ユニークな作品を通じて、様々なグラフィックスに活かせるアイデアが実感できる内容です。

The newest and most distinctive calendars from designers around the world. The collection features a variety of calendar types highly selected from numerous outstanding works ranging from standard wall calendars to unique pieces in form and design, including lift-the flap calendar, 3D calendar, pencil calendar and more.

949

GRAPHIC TOOLS IN SERVICE BUSINESSES
サービス業の案内グラフィックス

Page: 224 (Full Color)　¥14,000 + Tax

ハードウェアからソフトウェアへの移行にともなう通信関連業、既に定着した働く女性増加における代行業、高齢化社会における介護・医療業務など、社会は今、サービス業の需要が確実に増え、生活に欠かせないものとなっています。本書ではサービス内容を案内するカタログ・リーフレットを中心に、その他広告ツールも併せて紹介します。

The demands for service industries have become an indispensable part of life in the world today. This book looks at the sucessful campaigns of competitive service businesses ranging from telecommunications, internet, finance to restaurants, hotels and clinics. This is a good resource not only for designers but marketing professionals.

930

CORPORATE PROFILE & IMAGE
業種別 企業案内グラフィックス

Page: 256 (Full Color)　¥15,000 + Tax

本書は会社案内を中心に、学生が求める情報と使いやすさを熟慮した入社案内や、その企業の持つ個性を凝縮したコンセプトブック、会社のイメージアップにつながる企業広告などをさまざまな業種にわたり収録。単なる会社のスペック案内だけにとどまらない、企業理念やメッセージを社内外にわかりやすく的確に伝える、デザイン性に優れた作品を紹介します。

A collection of print materials that help create and support corporate image in a wide range of industries: company profiles as well as concept books designed to epitomize company character, corporate ads designed specially to improve company image, recruiting brochures, and more.

877

LOCAL BRAND DESIGN
地域ブランド戦略のデザイン

Pages: 224 (Full Color)　¥14,000 + Tax

地域特性を活かした商品・サービスのブランド化と地域イメージのブランド化を結びつけ、全国レベルのブランド展開を目指す「地域ブランド戦略」の取り組みが全国各地で積極的に行われています。本書ではデザイナーが地域ブランド戦略に関わることで認知度アップに成功した実例を紹介します。地方自治体のキャンペーン展開や目を引く特産品のパッケージ、ショップのグラフィックツールなどのアイテムを多数収録。

This title features the brand marketing strategies for products and services available only in the limited area in Japan. Each brand is created based on the unique identity for the local area, which draws peopleÅfs attention and leads to nationwide the brand recognition.

917

SALES STRATEGY AND DESIGN
販売戦略とデザイン

Page: 224 (Full Color)　¥15,000 + Tax

様々な業種の商品発売（サービス業の商品も含む）に伴う告知プロモーションを商品ごとに紹介。思わず手に取るネーミングや、店頭で目を引くパッケージ、消費者の心をくすぐるノベルティなど、各々のアイテムを巧みに利用した例を多数収録。

Unique and outstanding graphic tools in new product/service launching. Here are packages, novelties and the naming of product offering the newest communication styles to consumers!! With explanation of concept and motive for product / promotional tools.

790

販売戦略とデザインは、切っても切れない関係というのが、この本のあらすじです。

Sales Strategy and Design

NEW SHOP IMAGE GRAPHICS 2
ニュー ショップイメージ グラフィックス 2

Page: 224 (Full Color)　¥15,000 + Tax

お店の個性を強く打ち出すためには、販売戦略と明確なコンセプトに基づいた、ショップのイメージ作りが重要です。本書は様々な業種からデザイン性の高いショップアイデンティティ展開を、グラフィックツールと店舗写真、コンセプト文を交え紹介。

Second volume of the best seller titls in overseas. New Shop Image Graphics released in 2002. This book covers the latest, unique and impressive graphics in interiors and exteriors of various shops as well as their supporting materials.

789

SHOP IMAGE GRAPHICS IN LONDON
ショップイメージ グラフィックスイン ロンドン

Pages: 192 (Full Color)　¥9,800 + Tax

コンラン卿に影響を受けたモダンテイストのインテリアショップやデザインホテル、ユースカルチャーの中心的存在である音楽やアパレルショップ、ナチュラル志向のオーガニックレストランやスパ、エステなどロンドンならではの個性的なショップを厳選して紹介します。モダンな最新ショップからクラシカルな老舗店まで、今最もエキサイティングな都市ロンドンのショップアイデンティティ特集です。

Features 97 London shops and shows the intimate connection between the city's history and the street design, which's influenced internationally. The presented examples are dominated by these broad designs: classic, modern, and exotic.

933

ABSOLUTE APPEAL: DIRECT MAIL DESIGN
魅せる掴む DM デザイン

Page: 224 (Full Color)　¥14,000+Tax

ターゲットをつかむために様々な工夫が凝らされたDMを厳選し、その制作意図にまで踏み込んで紹介します。素材や形状など、取り上げたDMのポイントとなる部分をレイアウトで大胆に見せていくほか、デザインの狙いを文字情報で提供し、表現に込められた "戦略" を分かりやすくひも解きます。

This book introduces a variety of DM that have succeeded in captivating the target audience and winning their hearts. Many of the photos focus on the quality of the materials in an effort to provide the reader with a sense of what is the most distinguishing feature of DM, something that is normally gained only by picking them up and feeling them.

925

書き文字・装飾文字 グラフィックス

Page: 192 (Full Color)　¥9,800 + Tax

普段使われるフォントではなく、手書きや装飾された個性的な文字を使用したグラフィック作品を紹介。筆文字は力強く和のイメージを、ペン文字はラフでやさしいイメージを感じさせます。文字選びは作品のイメージを左右する重要なポイントです。

Sales in Japan only.

787

FOOD PACKAGE DESIGN
フードパッケージ デザイン

Page: 160 (Full Color) ￥7,800+Tax

ところ狭しと並んだ食品の棚で、いかに目を引き美味しそうにみえるか、インパクトと洗練されたデザインが求められるのが食品パッケージ。ショップのイメージと統一された戦略的デザインや、スーパーマーケットのオリジナルパッケージ、形の面白さを追求したパッケージなど、世界中から選りすぐった、新しい発想の食品パッケージを約400点紹介します。

896

A collection presenting a wide variety of packaging for foods from all corners of the world. The some 400 carefully selected works shown within are distinctive for their unified marketing strategies linked to product and store image, their interesting forms and use of color, their aesthetic pursuits and more.

COSMETICS PACKAGE DESIGN
コスメパッケージ & ボトル デザイン

Page: 160 (Full Color) ￥7,800 + Tax

化粧品、ヘルスケア用品（シャンプー・石鹸・入浴剤・整髪剤）のパッケージ、ボトルやチューブのデザインを中心に紹介。また、それらの商品しおり、ディスプレイ写真もあわせて掲載。「今、女性にウケるデザインとは？」がわかる1冊です。

526

Cosmetics and personal care products and their packaging represent the state of the art in design sensitive to the tastes of contemporary women. This collection presents a wide range of flowery, elegant, charming, and unique packages for makeup, skincare, body, bath, and hair-care products and fragrances selected from all over the world.

FREE PAPER GRAPHICS
フリーペーパー グラフィックス

Pages: 240 (Full Color) ￥14,000 + Tax

手軽な情報ツール・新しい広告媒体として注目される今話題のフリーペーパー。専門誌並みに詳しい内容のものから、ファッションやカルチャーなど市販雑誌に負けない充実した内容のものまで多種多様です。本書ではデザイン性の高い、優れたフリーペーパーを厳選し、総合情報・地域情報・専門情報の3つに分類して紹介しています。巻末には各誌の年間 "特集タイトル" を掲載。この1冊でフリーペーパーの "今" がわかります。

907

Free papers are fast becoming the talk of the industry as a new advertising medium and a more casual, inexpensive communications tool. This collection presents a carefully selected array of well-designed free papers grouped in three categories: general,

EARTH-FRIENDLY GRAPHICS
ロハス グラフィックス

Page: 240 (Full Color) ￥14,000+Tax

ロハス (LOHAS - life style of Health and Sustainability) とは地球環境保護と健康な生活を最優先し、人類と地球が共存できる持続可能なライフスタイルのこと。ここ数年で日本のロハス人口は増加し、ロハスをコンセプトにした商品の売れ行きは好調です。本書では地球と人にやさしい商品のコンセプトとともに広告・販促ツール・パッケージデザインまでを業種別のコンテンツにわけて分かりやすく紹介します。

902

"Earth-Friendly Graphics" is a collection of unique graphic communications including package design, promotional tools and advertising for environmental-friendly products and services based on the concept of Lifestyles of Health and Sustainability (LOHAS), the focus of increasing attention in recent years.

GUIDE SIGN GRAPHICS
ガイドサイン グラフィックス

Page: 272 (Full color) ￥14,000 + Tax

近年、さまざまな施設で見られる「ガイドサイン」。ユニバーサルを意識した病院の色彩デザインや、地方の私立大学の個性を活かしたインテリアサイン、その他、美術館や空港など、利用者の世代や使用言語が異なる人々が利用する施設にこそ、わかりやすい、優れたサインが見られます。本書は豊富な使用実例を見せながら、時代のニーズに合わせた国内と海外のサインシステムをご紹介します。

875

Sign systems are designed to meet the demands of the times. It's in facilities used by different ages, or speaking different languages, that the most user-friendly signage can be found. This book presents an extensive collection of photographs, examples of guide signs in practical use, and is an essential reference for designers.

URBAN SIGN DESIGN
最新 看板・サイン大全集（CD-ROM 付）

Page: 256 (Full Color) ￥15,000 + Tax

街を彩るさまざまな看板を飲食・製造・販売・サービスなど業種別にまとめて紹介。256ページのボリュームに加え、掲載写真の収録CD-ROMも付いた看板デザイン集の決定版。サイン業界のプロから、あらゆるクリエイターにお薦めしたい1冊です。

836

From among the many signs that flood city streetscapes, we've selected only the most striking, the most beautiful, the most tasteful, and present them here categorized by industry: restaurant, manufacturing, retail, and service. A whopping 256 pages of signs ranging from world-renowned brands to local restaurants, this single volume is sure to provide a source of ideas with a CD-ROM.

カタログ・新刊のご案内について

総合カタログ、新刊案内をご希望の方は、はさみ込みのアンケートはがきをご返送いただくか、下記ピエ・ブックスへご連絡下さい。

CATALOGS and INFORMATION ON NEW PUBLICATIONS

If you would like to receive a free copy of our general catalog or details of our new publications, please fill out the enclosed postcard and return it to us by mail or fax.

CATALOGUES ET INFORMATIONS SUR LES NOUVELLES PUBLICATIONS

Si vous désirez recevoir un exemplaire gratuit de notre catalogue généralou des détails sur nos nouvelles publication. veuillez compléter la carte réponse incluse et nous la retourner par courrierou par fax.

CATALOGE und INFORMATIONEN ÜBER NEUE TITLE

Wenn Sie unseren Gesamtkatalog oder Detailinformationen über unsere neuen Titel wünschen.fullen Sie bitte die beigefügte Postkarte aus und schicken Sie sie uns per Post oder Fax.

ピエ・ブックス

〒170-0005 東京都豊島区南大塚 2-32-4
TEL: 03-5395-4811 FAX: 03-5395-4812
www.piebooks.com

PIE BOOKS

2-32-4 Minami-Otsuka Toshima-ku Tokyo 170-0005 JAPAN
TEL: +81-3-5395-4811 FAX: +81-3-5395-4812
www.piebooks.com

ショップ イメージ グラフィックス イン パリ
Shop Image Graphics in Paris

2008 年 8 月 5 日　初版第 1 刷発行

Art Direction & Cover Design
セキユリヲ（エア）　Yurio Seki (ea)

Designer
松村大輔　Daisuke Matsumura

Editor
高橋かおる　Kaoru Takahashi

Editor & Coordinator (Paris)
鈴木春恵　Harue Suzuki

Photographers
物写真　　　　武田正彦　Masahiko Takeda
ショップ写真　鈴木春恵　Harue Suzuki

Illustrator
よしい ちひろ　Chihiro Yoshii

Translator
パメラ・三木　Pamela Miki

Publisher
三芳伸吾　Shingo Miyoshi

発行元　ピエ・ブックス
〒 170-0005　東京都豊島区南大塚 2-32-4
編集　TEL: 03-5395-4820　FAX: 03-5395-4821
　　　　e-mail: editor@piebooks.com
営業　TEL: 03-5395-4811　FAX: 03-5395-4812
　　　　e-mail: sales@piebooks.com
http://www.piebooks.com

印刷・製本　図書印刷株式会社